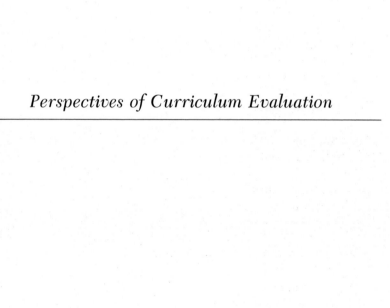

Perspectives of Curriculum Evaluation

AMERICAN EDUCATIONAL RESEARCH ASSOCIATION
MONOGRAPH SERIES
ON
CURRICULUM EVALUATION

Committee on Curriculum Evaluation:
Harold Berlak
Leonard S. Cahen
Richard A. Dershimer
Christine McGuire
Jack C. Merwin
Ernst Z. Rothkopf
James P. Shaver
Robert E. Stake

Coordinating Editor
Robert E. Stake

Editorial Associates:
J. Myron Atkin
Peter A. Taylor

Editorial Consultants for this Issue:
John B. Gilpin
J. Thomas Hastings
Thomas O. Maguire

American Educational Research Association
1126 Sixteenth Street, N. W.
Washington, D. C. 20036

Perspectives of
Curriculum Evaluation

Ralph W. Tyler

*Center for Advanced Study in the
Behavioral Sciences*

Robert M. Gagné

University of California, Berkeley

Michael Scriven

Indiana University

Rand McNally & Company
Chicago

RAND McNALLY EDUCATION SERIES

B. OTHANEL SMITH, *Series Editor*

Contents

Perspectives of Curriculum Evaluation

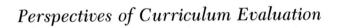

Toward a Technology for the
Evaluation of Educational Programs

"Let the buyer beware," declared the 19th-century individualist. What faith in human judgment! Then, as now, some "buyers" lacked the needed powers of judgment, but those who had them were expected to use them, and those who did not were said to deserve no concern. Yesteryear's spokesman for individualism advocated self-responsibility for one's choices and protested against government and consumer-collective action in the marketplace.

The marketplace in the last third of the 20th century will feature, along with provisions for sustenance, comfort, leisure, and longevity, a great array of products for the never-ending education of an inquisitive populace. Both government and private corporations have already initiated vast new production lines. Revolutionary curricula are emerging. Should the buyer beware? Can the buyer beware? What agencies are prepared to evaluate these educational products and programs? What steps should be taken to gain an understanding of an Operation Headstart or a school system designed by Litton Industries? We little understand the traditional operations of school systems. How can we understand the new?

How much we expect society to help the individual make decisions, in the marketplace and out, has changed greatly over the last 80 years. Most people now believe that government must not only protect against the grossly negligent and wanton, but must also license and standardize the conduct of legitimate business. Nongovernment agencies such as consumer organizations, professional associations, and producer self-regulatory bodies have been created to help provide information for judgment and decision.

How about the educational consumer? Can the teacher, superintendent, and curriculum coordinator choose wisely? Far too little information is now available. Little is known about the merit and shortcoming of products and programs. For excellence in

1

education we need excellent books and excellent teachers, but our methods of recognizing excellence are inadequate. For a few years, at least, there will be little quality control of goods produced by Research and Development Centers, by the growing curriculum-innovation projects, and by the newborn instruction industry. Much of the forthcoming educational output will be excellent, but not all. We grade the eggs a buyer cannot grade for himself and we legislate automobile safety standards. Yet far more crucially than eggs or automobiles, educational programs shape our future society. Should educational programs continue to escape formal evaluation?

ACCURACY VERSUS COMPLETENESS

"Let's call a spade a spade," declares a 20th century logical-positivist. What faith in perspicacity! To treat a spade properly we must recognize it as a spade. To specify the impact of an educational program we must be able to perceive impact.

Measurement specialists are proud of their perspicacity. "If it exists," they say, "it exists in quantity; and if it exists in quantity, it can be measured." It follows that if an educational program has an impact, that impact can be measured. Most specialists in educational testing and measurement believe they can do the job. The general public and most members of the educational profession presume that after having analyzed his data the "testing man" can state in precise terms the worth of a curriculum. The language of the Elementary and Secondary Education Act of 1965, Title I, implies that capability to evaluate is presently within our command. But the fluidity of our experiments and the bluntness of our tests deny us that capability. Neither quantity nor quality of impact is measured.

These are not, however, the greatest of our measurement problems: A spade is not just a spade. We do not have labels to identify each spade—and each educational program—so that it can be understood by label alone. Each needs ample description. Each differs from the others in a multitude of ways, and representation by title alone or by some composite score or rating leaves much of the story untold.

Our measurements are not perfectly accurate. We could devote ourselves to improving the precision of our instruments, but are there not higher-priority tasks? For the evaluation of curricula, I believe that we should postpone our concern for greater precision.

We should demonstrate first our awareness of a full array of teaching and learning phenomena. We should *extend* to this array our ability to observe and pass judgment. We should commit ourselves to a more *complete* description.

New techniques of observation and judgment need to be developed. In fact, we need a new technology of educational evaluation. We need new paradigms, new methods, and new findings to help the buyer beware, to help the teacher capitalize on new devices, to help the developer create new materials, and to help all of us to understand the changing educational enterprise.

PROFESSIONAL TOOLS AND TACTICS

It is not uncommon today for educational psychologists and measurement specialists to serve as advisors to evaluation projects. The inclination of these professionals, not surprisingly, is to use their most refined tools and techniques. Most of these tools and techniques were developed for differentiating among individual students, not for measuring the impact of an instructional program. Although differences in impact are indeed related to differences in student groups, curriculum evaluation and student evaluation require different measurement tactics.

Measurement consultants usually recommend specification of objectives in behavioral terms, experimental studies rather than status studies, and testing with instruments of empirically demonstrated reliability. Clearly these recommendations have their merit, but they can misguide evaluation efforts. J. Myron Atkin (1963) and Elliot Eisner (1966) have indicated how behavioral specification may disembody an educator's purpose. Lee Cronbach (1963) has indicated how a preoccupation with reliability can drain away an evolving test's content validity. Experimental controls are needed in the laboratory, regression equations are needed in the admissions office, and behavioral language is an essential consideration in test construction, but such techniques *may not* facilitate the conduct of an evaluation project.

Within the school, teachers and administrators evaluate their programs. Usually their purpose is self-improvement. When approaching the task in a formal way, they choose checklists and questionnaires as tools. Unfortunately, their inquiries are seldom validated, their attention to student achievement is negligible, and they seldom consider alternate ways of teaching. Still, these lay evaluations can be admired. They do attend to important facets of the situation that are absent from the reports of measurement experts. New measurement tools and tactics should be devised for what is of obvious concern to the lay evaluators.

The official accreditation agencies and accreditation associations of the nation have not accepted the role of evaluator. They have established certain minimum standards. Each standard is believed to be related to quality education. When a school is rated, the extent to which standards are met is indicated—but the real worth of its educational program is not apparent in an accreditation report.

What strategies and tactics are needed for real evaluation? The writers of these first monographs, Ralph Tyler, Robert Gagné, and Michael Scriven, urge more attention to diagnostic testing, to task analyses, and to evaluation of goals. The approaches they offer are not completely new, but the attempt to bring them together for curriculum evaluation is all too new. Some of us see in these techniques the beginnings of a technology of evaluation. Our guess is that this technology will draw from instructional technology, psychometric-testing technology, social-survey technology, communication technology, and others; and that it will become a contributor to the understanding of evaluation in areas other than education.

The skeptical reader may respond that neither new tactics nor new tools are needed—that available tools used in the right way can do the job. Later, I will try to show why we should not expect certain common tools to be useful for evaluation, but first I want to specify what I mean by "curriculum evaluation."

A DEFINITION OF CURRICULUM EVALUATION

A curriculum is an educational program. It can be informally organized: what a craftsman teaches an apprentice; or formally organized: what is taught in an instructional film. A curriculum, defined in this way, could be a mere lesson, or it could be the curricular program of a comprehensive high school, or the entire educational program of a nation. A curriculum may be specified in terms of what the teacher will do, in terms of what the student will be exposed to, or—as Gagné does in this issue—in terms of student achievement.

Educational programs are characterized by their purposes, their content, their environments, their methods, and the changes they bring about. Usually there are messages to be conveyed, relation-

ships to be demonstrated, concepts to be symbolized, under-
standings and skills to be acquired. Evaluation is complex because
each of the many characteristics requires separate attention.

(The purpose of educational evaluation is expository: to acquaint
the audience with the workings of certain educators and their
learners. It differs from educational research in its orientation to a
specific program rather than to variables common to many programs. A *full* evaluation results in a story, supported perhaps by
statistics and profiles. It tells what happened. It reveals perceptions
and judgments that different groups and individuals hold—
obtained, I hope, by objective means. It tells of merit and shortcoming. As a bonus, it may offer generalizations ("The moral of the
story is . . .") for the guidance of subsequent educational programs.

Curriculum evaluation requires collection, processing, and
interpretation of data pertaining to an educational program. For a
complete evaluation, two main kinds of data are collected: (1)
objective *descriptions* of goals, environments, personnel, methods
and content, and outcomes; and (2) personal *judgments* as to the
quality and appropriateness of those goals, environments, etc. The
curriculum evaluator has such diverse tasks as weighing the outcomes of a training institute against previously stated objectives,
comparing the costs of two courses of study, collecting judgments
of the social worth of a certain goal, and determining the skill or
sophistication needed for students commencing a certain scholastic
experience. These evaluative efforts should lead to better decision-
making: to better development, better selection, and better use of
curricula.)

SOME LIMITATIONS OF AVAILABLE TESTS

Most contemporary evaluations of instruction begin and end with
achievement testing. A large number of standardized tests are
available. Many of these tests have been developed with appropriate attention to the *Standards for Educational and Psychological
Tests and Manuals* (American Psychological Association, 1966)
and to such well-considered guidelines as those in *Educational
Measurements* (Lindquist, 1951, now in revision). It is important to
our concern here to emphasize that these tests have been developed to provide reliable discrimination among *individual students*.
Discriminability among students is important for instruction and
guidance, but for development and selection of curricula, tests are

needed that discriminate among curricula. Different rules for test administration are possible, and different criteria of test development are appropriate, when the tests are to be used to discriminate among curricula.

For the usual standardized achievement test, the test author writes a large number of "general-coverage" or "general-skill" items. If certain content areas are unlikely to be encountered by many students, the author avoids them. Items on special content, even when valid, show up poorly on item analyses, and are weeded out. Since the items of a standardized achievement test are meant to be fair to students of all curricula, they are aimed at what is common to all. By intent, the standardized achievement test is unlikely to encompass the scope or penetrate to the depth of a particular curriculum being evaluated.

Items having a strong relationship with general intelligence usually look good in an item analysis. These items correlate highly among themselves and moderately with almost any achievement items. Since they *are* indirect measures of achievement which successfully predict subsequent performance, they are accepted by teachers and counselors as well as test developers. But indirect measurement of achievement is irrelevant, even offensive, to many curriculum developers and supervisors of instruction. They want to know *what* has been learned. They want to know what deficiencies remain in student understanding. The standardized test does not tell them.

Apart from clinical experience, our only current basis for interpreting most test performances is the frequency distribution of "total-test" scores collected from a norm group. Reputable test publishers have been reluctant to endorse subtest scores or to provide item response information. Clearly, individual-student decisions resting on responses to one or just a few items are questionable. Unlike the counselor, the curriculum supervisor does not concentrate on individual-student decisions. He must explain the variance among curricula. Test developers could help him by providing item data or, better still, by constructing separate subtests for each specific curricular objective. That would be a departure from current practice.

Please do not misunderstand me. I am not belittling our standardized achievement tests. I am favorably impressed with their usefulness for counseling students. But they are not equally useful for evaluation. I am dismayed by my colleagues who believe that these same tests can be used to satisfy the needs of the curriculum evaluator.

SOME NEEDED THINKING

The evaluator needs a battery of standard operating procedures. Procedures depend on criteria. Criteria depend on rationales. Rationales depend on theories. From evaluation theory to practice, new thinking is needed.

Regarding curriculum development, we need standard ways of translating aims and needs into practices. Our measurement and programmed-instruction specialists have developed taxonomies of objectives. Our classroom-learning-laboratory personnel have developed principles of instruction governing sequences of rules and examples, schedules for practice and review, hierarchies of understanding, etc. But there is no "compiler language," no grand scheme for deriving educational activities from given objectives. We need lesson-writing paradigms, including subroutines for helping an author maintain a pace, control reading difficulty, organize review exercises, discover inconsistencies, optimize redundancies, etc. Things like these, done today intuitively by authors and editors, should be done more explicitly with routine check on the quality of the materials written.

Whether accomplished by author and editor or by author and computer, the derivation of lessons should be examined on logical grounds. Today the evaluator lacks a rational procedure for checking the logic of the development of a curriculum. He needs ways to measure the correspondence between the intent of a lesson plan and the original goal. Does it require a thorough understanding of the subject matter? Should he employ a logician? We do not know.

As a part of this evaluation, communication integrity should be considered. Much of education includes the conveying of a certain message to a student audience. From the time a message is conceived until the students are exposed to it, a considerable transformation of the message is likely to take place. Does the author say what he wants to say? Does the teacher say what the author intended him to say? This concern applies whether the author is a subject-matter expert, e.g., a nuclear physicist, or the final transmitter, e.g., the physics teacher himself. Some writings are more illuminating than others, some homework problems are more pertinent than others, some demonstrations are more applicable than others. Some teachers use the right words but obscure the message, others refine and extend the message. To understand one important quality of a curriculum we must appraise the fidelity of its communications.

We need techniques for representing the perspectives held by different people. Although they use the same language, different people see things differently. Do parents and the school board, consultants and the regular staff see things differently? Although two groups respond differently to a question, they may see the same merit in certain instruction. We need better devices for scaling perceptions of objectives. We need better procedures for processing judgments. At the beginning these procedures will not have the precision of an aptitude test or the elegance of an interest inventory, but even crude attempts to scale perceptions should be useful.

What are appropriate and inappropriate roles for the classroom teacher in curriculum evaluation? Can we capitalize upon the considerable ability of teachers to estimate which of two demonstrated teaching techniques is more likely to accomplish a particular long-term goal? Through training we could refine the teacher's powers of observation and estimation to make his contribution both technically sound and educationally valid. It is not unreasonable to conjecture that some day the primary role of the classroom teacher may be as a curriculum trouble-shooter, a conceptually oriented monitor, an evaluator—the essential link between the school's provision of a standard learning situation and the modification of it to accommodate the uniqueness of the student.

Several of the needs listed in this section call for psychometric thinking, the province of the psychologist. Other needs listed here and elsewhere call for help from the sociologist, the communications expert, the linguist, the philosopher, the anthropologist, and the economist. Can we find men of such pursuits to think with us as we develop our methodology of evaluation? I believe we must.

PRECURSORS OF A LITERATURE

Educational evaluation has not been without its champions. The social science literature includes many relevant works. A few will be cited here—more extensive coverage can be found in the bibliography.

Psychometric testing, for example, has been thoroughly discussed. For our purposes, the testing literature is nicely represented by *Educational Measurement* (Lindquist, 1951), with its farthest extension toward curriculum being Tyler's chapter on the measurement of learning. Among other fine writings on the evaluation of learning are those of Dressel and Mayhew, whose 1954 report is widely accepted as a textbook aimed at the evaluation of course offerings, and portions of Ahmann and Glock's *Evaluating Pupil Growth* (1963). Many measurement projects deserve attention, but only two reports will be mentioned here: Project TALENT (Flanagan, 1964) and the National Assessment of Educational Progress (Tyler, 1966).

Techniques for the evaluation of teaching directly apply to curriculum evaluation. Prominent among writings in this area are Gage's *Handbook of Research on Teaching* (1963), and publications of McKeachie (1959) and Simpson and Seidman (1962).

Conant (1959), Gardner (1961), and Trump (1960) have made thorough but nontechnical evaluations of the nation's schools. Defining educational goals for the nation has been a continuing undertaking of the Educational Policies Commission (1959, 1961). More immediate instructional objectives have been the concern of Bloom (1956), Krathwohl (1964), Lindvall (1964), and their colleagues. The study of educational decision-making has been relatively neglected, but noteworthy are the works of Cronbach and Gleser (1964) and James (1963).

School environments, notably college environments, have been the focus of study by Astin (1961) and Pace (1965-66). Benson (1961), Carlson et al. (1965), and Mort (see Mort and Furno, 1960) have considered economic and social aspects of school systems. Questions concerning curriculum development have been discussed extensively by Taba (1962) and in a collection edited by Heath (1964b). On the general topic of innovation in education, Clark and Guba (1965), Miles (1964), and Pellegrin (1966) are frequently cited.

Innovation in measurement methodology is apparent in the literature. Methods well established in other branches of educational research have found applications in curriculum evaluation. Psychological scaling (Torgerson, 1958), Osgood's semantic differential (1957), and Flanders' interaction analysis (1961) are examples. The Damrin-Glaser tab-testing methods, adapted for group testing by McGuire (1966), seem to have particular promise.

As Britton (1964) found, much of the literature relevant to curriculum evaluation exists in impermanent form—office papers, conference handouts, etc. Many valuable illustrative pieces are virtually unknown because they were written only for the persons concerned with a particular curriculum. City-wide and state-wide evaluations get little attention outside their jurisdiction, but some have generated documents and instruments worthy of wider distribution. Some of the more noteworthy studies have occurred in Baltimore, and in the states of New York, Pennsylvania, Florida, and California. Illustrative materials are sometimes available from consulting agencies such as the American Institute for Research; the Center for Instructional Research and Curriculum Evaluation at the University of Illinois; the Educational Testing Service; the Institute for Administrative Research at Teachers College, Columbia; and the Research and Development Center at UCLA.

THE CHALLENGE TO AERA

A professional organization sees no more clearly than its most sighted member, and seldom so well. Its actions usually serve more to consolidate rather than to extend, more to permit its members to tell of past deeds and future hopes than to propel them toward an institutional goal. So it has been with the American Educational Research Association.

It is possible for the more sighted members of almost any organization to become its officers. And so it has been with AERA.

In the early 1960's there were few independent sallies and little clamoring from the membership for the development of evaluation techniques. The officers of AERA, however, were then considering a possible impetus to evaluation efforts. They were aware that many new curricula were coming from such novel sources as National Science Foundation course-content improvement projects; that many special vocational programs were being initiated; that education had become a major instrument of war against poverty; and that the proliferation of programs now defies the local administrator's efforts to understand them on a personal basis.

Other professional organizations were also recognizing the need. The Association for Supervision and Curriculum Development, like AERA an affiliate of the National Education Association, devoted its Second National Conference on Curriculum Projects (Ammons and Gilchrist, 1965) to evaluation problems. The American Personnel and Guidance Association formed a subdivision called the Association for Measurement and Evaluation in Guidance. In 1965 a joint committee chaired by A. A. Lumsdaine and sponsored by AERA, the Department of Audio-Visual Instruction of the National Education Association, and the American Psychological Association prepared "Recommendations for Reporting the Effectiveness of Programmed Instruction Materials," a set of guidelines more general than the title suggests (Joint Committee on Programed Instruction and Teaching Machines, 1963). Note-worthy publications have been provided by the American Associa-tion of School Administrators, the American Council on Education, the National Citizens' Council for Better Schools, the National School Boards Association, and the National Association of Secon-dary School Principals. The need for evaluation has not escaped the attention of any of these professional organizations, but none commands the broad research purview or the measurement skill to apply to that need. AERA does.

None of the publications cited in these two sections strongly encourages the belief that curriculum evaluation can be accomp-lished by currently available tests, checklists, and visitation routines. New tools and techniques are needed. With its involve-ment in the development and refinement of educational curricula, AERA is in a unique position. More than any other professional organization, it faces the obligation, and the opportunity, to cul-tivate a methodology for the evaluation of education programs.

THE COMMITTEE ON CURRICULUM EVALUATION

In 1964 President Lee J. Cronbach appointed an ad hoc com-mittee to study possible AERA contributions. This committee, composed of N. L. Gage, Wells Hively II, John R. Mayor, and my-self, reported early in 1965 that a number of activities were war-ranted. It recommended in particular that a regular committee be named, that conferences be sponsored by AERA, and that a series of monographs be published.

Acting upon this report and upon his own perception of educa-tional affairs, President Benjamin S. Bloom in 1965 commis-sioned an AERA Committee on Curriculum Evaluation to develop guidelines for quality control—model evaluation procedures—to accompany the development and revision of educational curricula. Members of the 1965 committee were J. Stanley Ahmann, Leonard S. Cahen, Arthur Wells Foshay, Christine McGuire, Jack C. Merwin, Ernst Rothkopf, Richard A. Dershimer (ex officio), and myself. Harold Berlak and James P. Shaver were added in 1966 by President Julian C. Stanley. This committee, like its predecessor, concluded that guidelines limited to contemporary testing and inquiry procedures were inadequate; that special observation, data-reduction, and decision-making techniques were needed; and that AERA should encourage writing and discussion of theory and rationales for such techniques. As a first project, this Monograph Series was proposed. It was approved by the AERA Board of Directors early in 1966.

AERA, of course, has no writers of its own. The Monograph Series was created to attract contributions from members and non-members alike. Many disciplines should be represented. A distinguished educator, a distinguished psychologist, and a distinguished philosopher have contributed to this first issue. It is expected that economists, social anthropologists, communications specialists, school administrators, and classroom teachers will be among the authors of future issues.

Some issues will contain several monographs; most perhaps will be devoted to a single monograph. Attention will range across such diverse topics as decision-making, educational goals, innovation, merit in teaching, merit in textbooks, the measurement of change, content validity, the politics of education — in short, to any topic that contributes to the scholarly study and technical practice of evaluation in education.

This Monograph Series is not a new professional journal. It will be published aperiodically, to meet a current need. It will be continued only as long as the priority of the need remains high. The Series will exist as a medium for writings too lengthy and too elaborate for journal publication. It will include discourse. Some of this discourse will be speculative, some may even be supplicatory. Although some of the contributions will be theoretical and abstract, the ultimate purpose of the Series is to serve the practitioner. The primary criterion for acceptance of a manuscript will be whether, in the long run, what the author has to say will facilitate the development of palatable, comprehensive, and dependable evaluation procedures.

At this point, we do not know what directions this Monograph Series will take or what services it will render. Will it aid the curriculum developer? Will it ultimately help the buyer beware? We are convinced that the purposes of evaluation should be reconsidered, that our resources should be inventoried, that new models of evaluation should be proposed, and that new tactics should be discussed. The monographs in this Series should serve these ends.

ROBERT E. STAKE

Changing Concepts of Educational Evaluation

Ralph W. Tyler[1]

Center for Advanced Study in the Behavioral Sciences, Stanford, California

I have chosen this topic because it seems to me to deal with a problem likely to be faced in many areas of educational research as larger support enables us to move more rapidly and more comprehensively in developing scientific knowledge about education. My thesis is: The accelerating development of research in the area of educational evaluation has created a collection of concepts, facts, generalizations, and research instruments and methods that represent many inconsistencies and contradictions because new problems, new conditions, and new assumptions are introduced without reviewing the changes they create in the relevance and logic of the older structure.

To illustrate this, I should like to cite first our experience in the project concerned with assessing the progress of education. The purpose is to appraise the educational progress of large populations in order to provide the public with dependable information to help in the understanding of educational problems and needs and to guide in efforts to develop sound public policy regarding education. This type of evaluation is not focused upon individual students, classrooms, schools, or school systems, but is to furnish over-all information about the educational attainments of large numbers of people. Although the purpose is not identical with that of current achievement testing programs, we thought that available tests and/or test items would serve our purposes, but this turned out not to be the case.

Because current achievement tests seek to measure individual differences among pupils taking the tests, the items are concentrated on those which differentiate among the children. Exercises which all or nearly all can do, as well as those which only a

[1] A version of this paper was given as an invited address at the American Educational Research Association Annual Meeting, Chicago, February 17, 1966.

very few can do, are eliminated because these do not give much discrimination. But, for the purposes of assessing the progress of education, we need to know what all, or almost all, of the children are learning and what the most advanced are learning as well as what is being learned by the middle or "average" children. To obtain exercises of this sort is a new venture for most test constructors.

Because of the prevailing concept of measuring achievement in terms of the relative performance of individuals within a group, the difficulty level of test items is often manipulated by the item writer who changes the wording of the stem of the exercise, or of some of the multiple answers, without seeming to realize that in many cases this changes the nature of the behavior being appraised. Test practice and, to some extent, theory have been based on assumptions that are acceptable only for certain kinds of work.

We also find that little theory has been formulated or techniques devised to aid in the construction of relatively homogeneous samples of exercises faithfully reflecting an educational objective. The typical reliability coefficients refer to individual scores and not to the homogeneity of a given level of behavior. Our project will not compute individual scores, but the following sorts of things will be reported:

> For the sample of seventeen-year old boys of higher socioeconomic status from rural and small town areas of the Midwest region, it was found that:
>
> > 93% could read a typical newspaper paragraph like the following.
> > 76% could write an acceptable letter ordering several items from a store like the following.
> > 52% took a responsible part in working with other youth in playground and community activities like the following.
> > 24% had occupational skills required for initial employment.

Evaluation exercises on which such reports can be made must represent an acceptable degree of homogeneity so that, for example, the "newspaper paragraph" referred to above is typical of dozens of other paragraphs that are shown to represent the same difficulty level. We found that some people were interpreting current test items as though they were reliable samples of a given level of difficulty. Thus, reporters would comment on the fact that on a certain test only 12% of the students knew that Boise was the capitol of Idaho. If only 12% of those tested got this exercise right, this performance is likely to be idiosyncratic since neither do current tests seek to establish representative and reliable samples of what is known by only 12% of students nor do they comprehensively sample knowledge of state capitols. Our present instruments are products of assumptions and conditions that do not properly apply to some of our current needs for evaluation.

Another series of concepts, procedures, and instruments needs reexamination because of the current emphasis upon innovation at all levels of education. We can no longer depend so heavily upon the assumption that success in schools or colleges as they are now operating is an acceptable criterion for validating a measuring instrument. The task of the elementary school is now recognized as that of reaching all children, including the 15 to 20 per cent who have not been making appreciable progress in learning before. Our society can find constructive places for no more than 5 to 10 per cent of its people who are unskilled and untutored. The task of the high school is now recognized as that of educating a very large proportion of youth, including the 25 to 35 per cent who have not been making substantial progress in earlier years. The changing structure of the labor force, the higher requirements for intelligent citizenship both make this demand. Finally, the task of the college and university is to reach at least 50 per cent of our youth in order that our complex, industrial society can continue to develop.

These demands make untenable the assumption that there is a large pool of humanity from which the cream is to be skimmed off for certain educational or occupational purposes, and that failures in educational institutions are principally due to poor selection of students. On the other side of the coin, we now see that schools and colleges, like other institutions, become program-centered, losing their orientation toward their clients. Most institutions begin as responses to the need of certain clients for services. As years go by, programs are developed that are reasonably acceptable to the clients they have been serving. Then the institution is likely to believe that its program is its raison d'être rather than the need for its services. When this program-worship stage is reached, the institution seeks to find clients who like the program and can get along with it, and to deny admission to others. After a time, the terminology develops that those not admitted are "poor students," "not intelligent," not of "college calibre." In many cases, as in the founding of the Land-Grant Colleges, new institutions have to be established to serve the clients rejected by the older ones.

The current climate in this country is to seek innovation, to get the institutions active in learning how to serve their new clients. Evaluative instruments for this purpose must avoid using criteria based upon the current judgments of schools and colleges because this criterion perpetuates the conviction that these institutions are, at present, satisfactory for the tasks to be done.

In place of the older criteria and the dependent procedures we need new concepts of educational readiness, strengths on which to build, deficiencies to be attacked, and the like. These new concepts must be based on the assumption of dynamic potential in all or almost all human beings. The evaluation task is to describe or measure phases of this potential and difficulties to be surmounted that can help the individual and the educational institution in improving student learning.

This raises still another area for reexamination, the uncritical use of various forms of factor analysis. When Truman Kelley wrote his monumental volume, *Crossroads in the Mind of Man* (1928), nearly 40 years ago, scientific studies of human heredity were very limited. Hence, it was not a result of gross anti-intellectualism or ignorance that many psychologists and educators thought of factors as something inherent in the neural mechanism. However, this type of naïvete still continues in spite of the great advances that are being made in the sciences of human genetics and neurology. Because many of us think of "factors" obtained from tests as indicators of basic neural connections rather than as learned similarities or generalizat:ons, we tend to use factor scores or to restrict the range of types of evaluation exercises in cases where they are not appropriate or may be misleading, as well as in cases where their employment increases the efficiency of measurement.

Related to this is the changing conception of the plasticity and educability of human organisms generally. The initial work on transfer of training has left a legacy in which both teaching and testing are frequently based on a stochastic concept of learning. The earlier work of Judd (1921), Freeman (1917), and their students on generalization and teaching for transfer was largely overlooked until the emphasis given more recently by Bruner (1960) and others on the structure of the disciplines and the organized nature of cognitive learning. In both theory and practice, we who work on educational evaluation are still guided by procedures and instruments that treat items as units and learning measures largely as the sum of specific, unorganized bits.

The whole area of diagnostic testing has largely been neglected in practice although much of the basic theory was outlined in the milestone volume *Educational Measurement*, edited by E. F. Lindquist and published by the American Council of Education (Lindquist, 1951). In its Chapter 1, pp. 37-38, the late Walter Cook listed the following general criteria for diagnostic tests:

(1) They must be an integral part of the curriculum, emphasizing and clarifying the important objectives. (2) The test items should require responses to be made to situations approximating as closely as possible the functional. (3) The tests must be analytical and based on experimental evidence of learning difficulties and misunderstandings. (4) The tests should reveal the mental processes of the learner sufficiently to detect points of error. (5) The tests should suggest or provide specific remedial procedures for each error detected. (6) The tests should be designed to cover a long sequence of learning systematically. (7) The tests should be designed to check forgetting by constant review of difficult elements, as well as to detect faulty learning. (8) Pupil progress should be revealed in objective terms.

In Chapter 9 of that volume, pp. 266-67, Frederick Davis, in discussing item selection, comments:

> The difficulty of individual items is not an important consideration when items are selected for mastery tests.... Mastery tests are not intended to provide scores that will rank students in terms of their knowledge or ability; rather they are designed to separate students into two groups, those who know certain basic facts, principles or operations, and those that do not know them. For this reason, the items in a mastery test are so chosen that nearly every pupil who has reached a predetermined level of achievement can answer them all correctly.

In spite of these published statements, there are very few tests available meeting these conditions for diagnostic purposes. Now that high-speed computers and electronic data processing make individual diagnosis, recording, and treatment feasible, teachers do not have appropriate evaluation instruments to guide greater individualization of instruction. We are still so obsessed with the ranking of individuals on the basis of scores that we have not developed adequately the tools and procedures required. Theory and practice need to be reexamined in terms of present conditions and opportunities.

Perhaps the most basic assumptions we make in educational evaluation are those that deal with our concept of the role of the learner in learning and related notions about the nature of knowledge. If we conceive of the learner as one who is learning to make appropriate responses to situations outside his control, we are likely to think of learning as a kind of conditioning in which the only choice open to the learner is to react "correctly" or to refuse to respond. On the other hand, learning may be viewed as a process by which the learner develops a behavior that enables him to deal satisfactorily with the situation which he confronts in a way that more nearly achieves his purposes. The cartoon showing one rat telling another that he has got the psychologist under control because the psychologist gives him food whenever he presses a lever, seems humorous to us, but it illustrates the possibility of the learner devising ways to manipulate the situations he encounters rather than views him as one who must respond as the text or test requires or be penalized.

John Dewey was speaking of this when he characterized a good learning situation as one which requires the learner to make certain adaptations to those conditions beyond his control and to modify other conditions so as to serve his ends. Dewey considered a situation in which there was no freedom for the learner to reconstruct conditions as uneducative, as was also one in which he could manipulate all conditions according to his whim or fancy.

Related to this is the unstated view about knowledge. Is knowledge something "out there" which we must find out, remember, and follow, or is knowledge a product of human efforts to make sense out of the world, to accomplish certain tasks and to enhance human satisfactions? Knowledge as a continuing human effort is something which the learner must help to construct.

These different conceptions make a difference in the way achievement test exercises are designed, the directions written, and the "response-set" stimulated. We have not recently reviewed our theory and practice in educational evaluation to assure ourselves that they are in harmony with the basic assumptions on which current educational programs are operating.

The illustrations that I have been presenting are not exhaustive, but I hope that they have provided some indication of the meaning of the thesis with which I began—{"The accelerating development of research in the area of educational evaluation has created a collection of concepts, facts, generalizations, and research instruments and methods that represent many inconsistencies and contradictions because new problems, new conditions, and new assumptions are introduced without reviewing the changes they create in the relevance and logic of the older structure."} Before this mixed vegetation becomes a jungle, can we not establish the equivalent of the Physical Science Study Committee to sort out and arrange our materials in a more ordered fashion, eliminating obsolete notions, clarifying and strengthening the framework of our field?

Curriculum Research and the Promotion of Learning

Robert M. Gagné[1]

University of California, Berkeley

The central focus for change in educational practice during the past decade has been the curriculum. To be reminded of this fact, one hardly needs to mention the development of "modern mathematics," of the "new physics," the "new biology," and a great many other efforts of somewhat lesser fame but possibly equal importance. Curriculum revision has been carried out, and is still being pushed forward, by dedicated groups of university scholars, teachers, and educational researchers. It has progressed despite the well-known inertia of the schools, and the occasional grumbling of parents, so that quite a considerable totality of change has been effected in the course offerings of public schools from the twelfth grade down to the kindergarten. In all probability, we have not yet seen the asymptote of a curve of change for the curriculum.

With all due credit to these marvelous accomplishments, there are those who see dangers ahead. Sizer (1965), for example, states his belief that curriculum reforms are in danger of becoming accepted as gospel by the unwary. He sees a number of shortcomings in the curriculum development movement, not the least of which is the absence of systematic investigations of the effects of introduction of new curricula and courses of study.

Sizer's statement of the need for a greater amount of "scholarly rigor" in the whole process of curriculum development falls upon a set of sympathetic ears, so far as I am concerned. The questions I should like to address here are of the following sort: How can one test the principles used in curriculum design by empirical methods? What kinds of evidence can be sought to determine the extent to which a curriculum promotes the learning expected of it? Is it possible to use experimental methods to search for optimal "structure" and "sequence" in curriculum development? What dimensions of a curriculum may be varied in systematic experiments to determine their effects on students' learning?

[1]This paper was originally given as an invited address at the American Educational Research Association Annual Meeting, Chicago, February 18, 1966.

DEFINING THE CURRICULUM

By some educational writers, the curriculum is defined in a fairly broad way. For example, Taba (1962, p. 12) considers curriculum design as including (1) diagnosing educational needs; (2) formulating objectives; (3) selection of content; (4) organization of content; (5) selection of learning experiences; (6) organization of learning experiences; and (7) determining the ways and means of evaluating effectiveness of what is taught. Obviously, this is a very comprehensive definition of the domain of curriculum development, which encompasses questions of learning methods and instructional techniques as well as those of educational measurement.

There is much to be said for a broad definition of this sort. Particularly, it might be recommended to those aggregations of scholars in specific disciplines who have set out to improve existing curricula or to design new ones. Have they diagnosed the need? Have they formulated objectives? Have they faced the problem of selecting and organizing effective conditions of learning? And have they taken pains to insure that a reasonable evaluation of their new curriculum is possible? In some instances, of course, design of new curricula has in fact been carried out in a way that gives suitable consideration to all of these questions. In other instances, it has not, and the effects of this neglect will become increasingly apparent as time goes on.

For present purposes, however, I want to adopt a somewhat narrower definition of the curriculum, one that leaves out specific consideration of the design of learning conditions. This subject is the focus of interest of a recently published book (Gagné, 1965b). The problem I do want to discuss pertains to the relation of learning to the *selection and organization of content.* Does a particular item of content at some point in a curriculum facilitate learning or slow it up? Is there a sequence of curricular elements that promotes learning more than does some other sequence? And how can one find out?

DESCRIBING CONTENT

As is usually the case, if one is interested in finding dependable answers to such questions, it is necessary first to define terms. The most important terms involved here are *content, curriculum,* and the items of which the latter is built, which may be called curricular *units*.

What is meant by content? Is it something that has its existence on a printed page of text, in chapter headings, in the oral instruction of a teacher, or in the student's head? Each of these possibilities has some obvious difficulties. If content is the pages of a textbook, the definition would seem to be incomplete in leaving out much that is imparted by the teacher, or by other sources. Similarly, what the teacher says would be an incomplete representation of content for the same reason. Chapter headings may come a little closer to a comprehensive meaning, but surely they are not detailed enough to constitute a workable definition. What is in the student's head, assuming it can be determined, has the difficulty of being an outcome of the educational process rather than an input, as one ordinarily considers content to be.

A more satisfactory conception of content is as related to the goals of instruction, rather than to its effects. When so conceived, content must reflect goals that are independent of the media of instruction, whether these are the communications of a teacher, a textbook, or a television set. If the goals of instruction are involved in content, these must also be tied to the student's behavior, or perhaps to his expected behavior. These considerations lead to the idea that content needs to be stated as *objectives*, and that these objectives mean things that the student is able to accomplish. More specifically, content may be defined as *descriptions of the expected capabilities of students in specified domains of human activity*. It is important to note that such descriptions do not specify the expected behavior of the teacher, nor do they refer to the words in a textbook. They are descriptions of what the student is expected to be capable of doing, following some particular period of learning.

Defining objectives is a familiar requirement to educators and to educational researchers. Its importance to educational planning and the measurement of achievement has been emphasized by Tyler, Bloom, and others (Tyler, 1950, 1964; Bloom et al., 1956). The purposes that objectives may serve in teacher-student communication and in the design of instructional conditions have been pointed out in my own writings (Gagné, 1965a, 1965c).

Possibly the most fundamental reason of all for the central importance of defining educational objectives is that such definition makes possible the basic distinction between content and method. It is the defining of objectives that brings an essential clarity into the area of curriculum design and enables both educational planners and researchers to bring their practical knowledge to bear on the matter. As an example of the kind of clarification which results from defining content as "descriptions of the expected capabilities of students," the following may be noted. Once objectives have been defined, there is no step in curriculum design that can legitimately be entitled "selecting content." This is because the capabilities of the learner are directly derivable from the objectives themselves, as when from the objective "adds fractions" one derives the content statement "capability of adding fractions." One can select textbooks, motion pictures, laboratory equipment, even teachers; but one does not select content. It is derived from objectives, in a manner which will be discussed more fully in a moment.

What is a *unit* of content? First of all, it is a specific description of a single student capability. The difficulty in defining it derives from the fact that it is not a constant entity for all parts of a curriculum. In fact, the size of a unit has to vary with the particular content with which one is dealing, as this in turn is related to the capabilities of the student *prior* to his becoming involved with the objective being specified. Many examples could be given of this fact. For the six-year-old, who must learn to write, the description "prints the letters E and F" may at one point constitute a unit of content. For a nine-year-old, however, such a unit would normally be quite inappropriate, since he has already acquired a capability of "printing words," or "printing sentences." At one stage of instruction in mathematics, a reasonable unit may be "finding common factors in numerator and denominator," whereas at a later stage, this degree of specificity may be replaced by the unit "simplifying fractions."

Thus, a unit of content may be defined as *a capability to be acquired under a single set of learning conditions*, among these conditions being certain specified prerequisite capabilities. Newton's second law, for example, which is a principle relating mass, acceleration, and force, may be a unit of content provided the student has previously learned the concepts which make it up: in other words, if he already knows what is meant by mass, by acceleration, by force, by the equals sign, and by a product. If he has *not* acquired these concepts previously, then of course they must be taught. By derivation from the primary objective "ability to demonstrate Newton's second law," they themselves become units to be learned.

At this point it is possible to approach a definition of the word curriculum, which combines the idea of unit of content with the idea of prerequisites. *A curriculum is a sequence of content units arranged in such a way that the learning of each unit may be accomplished as a single act, provided the capabilities described by specified prior units (in the sequence) have already been mastered by the learner.* It is evident from this definition that a curriculum may be of any length, that is, it may contain any number of units. A curriculum is specified when (1) the terminal objectives are stated; (2) the sequence of prerequisite capabilities is described; and (3) the initial capabilities assumed to be possessed by the student are identified.

Figure 1 illustrates a curriculum of relatively circumscribed scope which may be called "the addition of integers" (Gagné, Mayor, Garstens, and Paradise, 1962). Notice that the terminal objectives, both of them, are stated. The sequence of prerequisite capabilities is specified. One can learn from the chart, for example, that the capability of "supplying other names for positive integers in statements of equality" (IIa) can be learned as a single act if the prior capability "stating and using the definition of addition of an integer and its additive inverse" (IIIa) has already been developed. The pattern of prerequisite capabilities for one of the terminal objectives (adding integers) is quite different, and shorter, than the sequence required for the other terminal objective (making a logical demonstration of the addition of integers). Finally, one can readily suppose that the capabilities at the lowest level of the chart are actually initial capabilities assumed to be present in the particular students for which this curriculum was designed.

DERIVING SUBORDINATE CAPABILITIES

How is it possible to derive a chart like this by working backwards from the terminal objectives shown at the top? In other articles (Gagné, 1962; Gagné, Mayor, Garstens, and Paradise, 1962) I have stated this to be a matter of asking the question of each task, "What would the learner have to know how to do in order to perform this task, after being given only instructions?" Such a statement can be elaborated somewhat with the use of the terms just previously defined. In order to find the *prerequisites* of a given unit of content, one needs to identify those units of previously acquired capabilities which would permit the learning of the given unit under a single set of learning conditions.

Stated in another way, units of the curriculum subordinate to each major objective may be derived by subjecting this objective

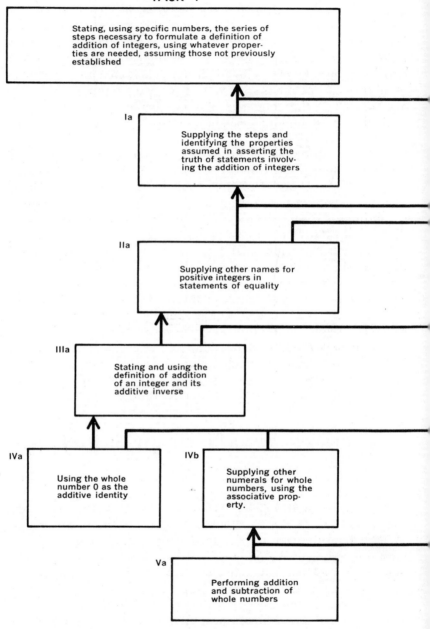

Figure 1. A curriculum hierarchy on the addition of integers (From Gagné,
Mayor, Garstens, and Paradise, 1962).

TASK 2

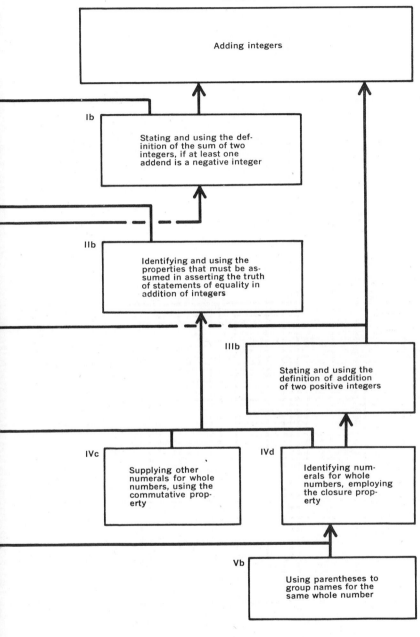

Adding integers

Ib Stating and using the definition of the sum of two integers, if at least one addend is a negative integer

IIb Identifying and using the properties that must be assumed in asserting the truth of statements of equality in addition of integers

IIIb Stating and using the definition of addition of two positive integers

IVc Supplying other numerals for whole numbers, using the commutative property

IVd Identifying numerals for whole numbers, employing the closure property

Vb Using parentheses to group names for the same whole number

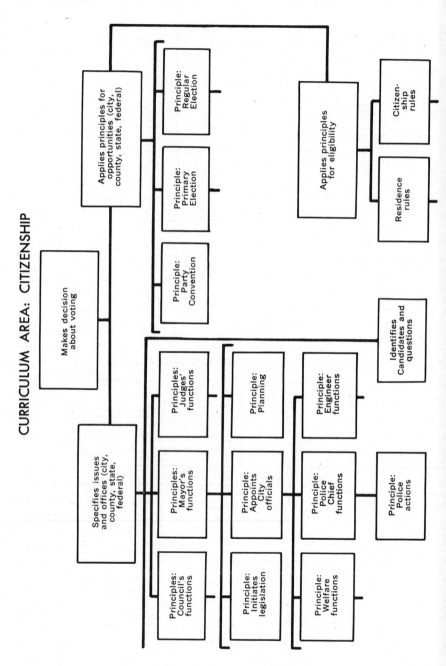

Figure 2. An incomplete curriculum hierarchy in the field of citizenship.

to analysis. It is a kind of *task analysis* (cf. Gagné, 1965b, 1965c), to give it a name developed in another context. The procedure is one which takes into account both (1) the components of a given objective and (2) the unity of the capabilities so defined, from the standpoint of learning conditions required to establish them. By progressively applying this analysis procedure beginning with the terminal objective and working backwards, one can spell out an entire structure of knowledge which has its beginning in relatively simple capabilities that can be assumed to be known by the student.

I am sometimes asked whether this kind of analysis can be applied to many sorts of subject matter, or does it require a subject like mathematics? I believe it is widely applicable to just about any subject, although it seems to me that some are tougher than others to analyze. A key to ease of analysis, however, is good objective statements of human performance. With a terminal objective like "Understands the origins of the American Revolution," one scarcely knows how to begin. But should the statement, "States the sequences of events relating six major causes to the American Revolution," be acceptable, the process of analysis is considerably simplified.

Another example is included in Figure 2, in the curriculum area of citizenship. The whole of this structure would be quite complex, and I am able to illustrate only a part of it here. Briefly, it may be read as follows. The terminal behavior is making a decision to vote or not to vote (which I assume every good citizen does). This decision is based upon three major sets of principles shown in the next row: the issues and offices; the opportunities for voting; and the rules for voter eligibility. The remainder of the structure on the left assumes that local offices are the focus of interest. In order to learn to specify issues, the learner must first learn the functions of council, mayor, and judiciary. In order to learn these functions, the learner must first acquire principles on initiating legislation, appointing city officials, and others. In order to learn the principles pertaining to appointing city officials, the learner must identify who they are, including the police chief. In order to learn the police chief's responsibilities, the learner must know what kinds of actions the police take. By this time one is getting fairly close to simple and general knowledge, and I stop here, emphasizing again the incomplete nature of the chart. It will be apparent that important additional sequences of units could be added by modern scholars of the social sciences.

OTHER CURRICULUM ANALYSES

A number of investigators have tried out this procedure and found it generally satisfactory. In published studies of my own and my co-workers, it has been applied to curricula dealing with number series (Gagné, 1962), solving equations (Gagné and Paradise, 1961), and elementary geometry (Gagné and Staff, Univ. of Md. Mathematics Project, 1965; Gagné and Bassler, 1963), besides the adding of integers already mentioned.

Other investigators have used basically similar methods of analyzing curricula. Glaser (1962) has described a number of different approaches to the analysis of instructional objectives to define a "learning structure," which is, of course, the same thing as a curriculum as defined here. Hively (1963) carried out an analysis of programmed instructional material on elementary mathematical operations with sets. Still another curriculum in mathematics was prepared by Kersh (1965) using what is called the TRAC procedure, involving principles highly similar to those previously described. An excellent example of the application of the method, again in connection with programmed materials, is contained in a report by Schutz, Baker, and Gerlach (1964). These investigators prepared careful analyses for three different terminal objectives: (1) capitalizing words in context; (2) adding and subtracting common fractions; and (3) inserting punctuation marks in unpunctuated text. These authors made special note of the fact that the curricula defined in this way differed considerably in their structure from those implied by the textbooks they examined. They also found a lack of correspondence between measures designed for subtopics in their structures and those of standard tests pertaining to these terminal objectives.

Mention should also be made of the analysis described by Eleanor Gibson on the subject of learning to read (E. J. Gibson, 1965). Gibson assumes that children approach this task with certain previously learned capabilities in communication, including speaking and understanding spoken language, employing language units organized with a grammatical structure. Under these assumptions, she identifies three major stages of learning, which are roughly sequential, in acquiring skill in reading. These are (1) learning to identify graphic symbols, (2) learning to decode letters into sounds, and (3) using progressively higher-order units of structure. Gibson's paper contributes much clarity to the problem of defining the behavioral meaning of these hierarchically ordered stages of learning to read, and identifies some of the basic research questions associated with each stage.

TESTING THE EFFECTIVENESS OF CURRICULA

Perhaps sufficient examples have been cited to establish the fact that determining the content and sequence of a curriculum can be based upon a rational analysis; and further, that such a procedure has been used to generate curricula that are highly satisfactory from the standpoint of their structural completeness. Of course this is not the end of the story. What one really wants to know about a given curriculum is whether it works. In more precise terms, one is interested in finding out whether learning is promoted by the presentation of particular content in a particular sequence.

A fairly straightforward method can be employed to test the appropriateness of a proposed curricular structure. This consists in designing and administering a test which has been specially constructed to yield pass-fail information on each knowledge unit within a total hierarchy. The data from such a test are then analyzed to reveal the sequential dependence of one unit on another. It may be noted that the test need not be given to students who have been instructed in accordance with a particular hierarchy — that is a later step in curriculum evaluation. But the test does need to be given to a group of students who have been exposed to instruction in the area identified by the hierarchy. That is to say, the instruction of the students to be tested should include the terminal objectives stated in the knowledge hierarchy under investigation.

In designing such a test, a couple of items are written to assess each unit of knowledge identified in the hierarchy. Two items are used for each, rather than one, in order to insure accuracy of measurement — after all, it is easy to write a bad item, which doesn't measure what it's supposed to. Basically, though, each item is designed to test whether the student can or cannot exhibit the performance implied by each unit capability in the hierarchy. It may be noted that the concept of difficulty is not relevant to such items. They should be neither easy nor difficult, but simply designed to measure what the student can or cannot do in terms of what is stated as an objective. Variations in difficulty, under such assumptions, are simply an indication that the items are ambiguously worded, inaccurately stated, or incorrectly administered; in other words, they are bad items.

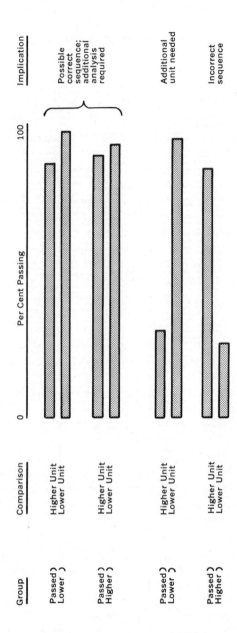

Figure 3. Hypothetical test results from groups of students on a higher and a lower knowledge unit in a curriculum sequence. The groups are first categorized into those who passed the higher unit, and those who passed the lower unit.

Having constructed a test to cover the entire knowledge hierarchy along these lines, the investigator then gives the test to a group of students who are supposed to have recently learned the domain of knowledge that the hierarchy identifies. The test should also be given to a group of students who have *not* had such instruction, in order that units can be identified which are *already learned*. In the description that follows, I shall assume that this initial step has already been taken, so that when a high percentage of students attains a unit correctly, it may be inferred that they have recently learned this unit, not that they already had it in their repertoire before the instruction was given. The data from such an administration may be analyzed to reveal the dependence of one unit of the curriculum on another. Figure 3 indicates some of the reasoning that enters into such an analysis.

First, one may look at the kinds of comparisons of adjacent knowledge units required by the analysis. Assume that one unit has been placed higher than another unit, so that, by hypothesis, the learning of the higher unit depends upon mastery of the lower unit. Did all, or nearly all, of those students who passed the higher unit also pass the lower? And did all, or nearly all, of those students who passed the lower unit pass the higher? These first two comparisons are indicated in the first four rows of Figure 3. Notice that the implication is that there *may* be a correct sequence here. However, it must be noted that these two units, called "higher" and "lower," may actually have a coordinate relation to each other; they both may depend upon a third unit in the same way. Therefore, an additional step in the analysis must be taken, to see how each behaves with respect to the *next lower* unit in the sequence. This additional analysis makes possible a determination of whether they are dependent one on another, or whether they both depend upon a third and lower unit.

The next row in the figure indicates a pretty clear determination. For the group of students who passed the lower unit, we find only a few who passed the upper unit. The meaning is quite obvious. These students were unable to progress to the higher unit from their knowledge of the lower unit. As for the proposed curriculum hierarchy, this means that one or more additional units must be inserted between the higher and lower unit.

The final row presents another situation having a clear implication. In this case, of the group that were able to complete the unit tested as "higher," only a few were able to pass the unit called "lower." Clearly, the ability to pass the higher unit did not, according to this result, depend upon the possession of what was hypothesized as the "lower" capability. Therefore, these units are incorrectly arranged in sequence.

These, then, are the kinds of analysis that appear to be needed to determined whether a *feasible sequence* of curriculum units has been planned. Table 1 indicates another tabulation of data that may be made as a result of the administration of a test of the sort described. This is simply a frequency distribution of the units correctly attained by a group of subjects. The table arranges five units in a hypothesized order indicated by Roman numerals, and indicates by an x the correct attainment of these units by each of ten

TABLE 1

HYPOTHETICAL DISTRIBUTIONS OF PASSING (x) BY
10 STUDENTS OF 5 SEQUENTIAL UNITS OF A CURRICULUM,
AS ARRANGED IN AN INITIAL TRY, AND IN A
REARRANGEMENT OF SEQUENCE

Students	Initial Try: Units					Students	Rearrangement: Units				
	I	II	III	IV	V		I	II	IV	III	V
1	x	x	x	x	x	1	x	x	x	x	x
2	x	x	x	x	x	2	x	x	x	x	x
3	x	x	x	x		3	x	x	x	x	
4	x	x	x	x		4	x	x	x	x	
5	x	x		x		5	x	x	x		
6	x	x		x		6	x	x	x		
7	x	x				7	x	x			
8	x	x				8	x	x			
9	x					9	x				
10	x					10	x				

students. The initial administration, it is supposed, yielded the data on the left. It may be noted that something is wrong with the sequencing of Units III and IV, since it is found that students 5 and 6 can attain Unit IV but not Unit III. When these are rearranged as in the right-hand part of this lower table, however, the sequence comes out right. The implication is that Unit IV should actually precede Unit III in a properly sequenced curriculum.

Some investigators have applied to data of this sort the method suggested by Guttman (1944) for scaling qualitative data, including a statistic called the reproducibility coefficient. It seems to me that this is an entirely reasonable application of this statistic, and that one may correctly employ Guttman's method in dealing with data of this sort. However, I need to point out that this method does not provide an analysis as discriminating as that described previously and illustrated in Figure 3. Particularly, it does not provide a means of distinguishing between a subordinate relationship and a co-ordinate one, as I have described these earlier. I fully realize that the type of analysis suggested in Figure 3 is not traditional in the field of achievement testing. But it seems to be in essence what is required in order to draw the desired conclusions about curriculum sequence. Perhaps someone with greater facility in quantitative analysis than I will be able to give it a greater elegance.

One additional point should be made concerning the use of this method to provide information about the sequence of a curriculum. It should be particularly noted that such a method does not provide an *evaluation* of a curriculum. It tells us merely whether a given hypothesized sequence is pedagogically reasonable, or feasible. It does *not* tell us how good the curriculum is. For the latter purpose, there is of course no shortcut method. One must actually put the curriculum into use, and then measure the results in terms of student achievement, or of some other specified criterion.

SOME EXAMPLES OF THE METHOD

The method I have described as a means of testing the appropriateness of a curriculum sequence has been employed in quite a variety of studies, ranging over several kinds of content. I have already mentioned some of my own work, and that of my colleagues. Hively's work (1963), also referred to previously, used the method to test several forms of curricula on finite sets, including the notions of "universe," "complement," "intersection," and "union." Schutz, Baker, and Gerlach (1964) carried out an elegant and comprehensive set of experiments using the method to reveal gaps, inversions, and unnecessary units in curricula on capitalization, fractions, and punctuation. Their results are of great importance to this field of research. Newton and Hickey (1965) used the method to test the feasibility and effectiveness of two different curriculum sequences concerned with economic principles of the Gross National Product. Smith and Moore (1965) explored the sequencing of curriculum units in programmed materials on Chinese History, Programmed Instruction, Logic Sentences, Federal Relations in Education, the Russian Alphabet, and Set Theory. Their findings support the notion that appropriate sequencing can be revealed by properly designed tests in these content areas. Cox and Graham

(1966) found that tests given to young children on adding two-digit numerals revealed both correct and incorrect sequences within a curriculum, and made possible the design of a hierarchy of tasks which exhibited a coherent structure having a high coefficient of reproducibility.

One other application of the method deserves particular mention, because it is an instance of considerable practical importance. I refer to the development of a curriculum in science for the elementary grades, by the American Association for the Advancement of Science, entitled *Science—A Process Approach*. This curriculum contains a number of exercises on each of the scientific processes of observation, classification, measurement, quantification, prediction, and inference, which are designed to build upon each other in the way that a good curriculum should. The scientists and educators who developed this program were following a sequence which was at first specified in only an approximate sense. Then, after the individual exercises were developed in accordance with the ingenuity of teams of writers, they were put together to form a sequence which seemed to be a reasonable one, beginning with the simpler forms of behavior and building to the more complex ones. Obviously, there is much chance of error in such an enterprise—it is fairly easy to get a unit out of place, or to imagine that one is subordinate to another when it really isn't. This particular curriculum sequence, however, has been tried out in a number of schools throughout the country. Since the testing of achievement on each unit was planned as an integral part of the program, considerable data have been collected, and some results have already been reported (AAAS Commission on Science Education, 1965). These data demonstrate the applicability of the method I have described to the problem of determining appropriateness of a curriculum sequence in elementary science.

IMPLICATIONS FOR RESEARCH

The general implications of these techniques and the findings they have yielded to date seem to be pretty clear. Let me state those that seem to me to have the broadest import.

1. The design of a curriculum, by which is meant the appropriate sequencing of units of content, can be based upon empirical evidence. It doesn't have to be a matter of speculation about what students are capable of learning, on the one hand, nor a matter of elegance of logical derivation, on the other. The pedagogical cor-

rectness of a sequence of content units can be tested by successively applied trials of what students can actually achieve. Initially, such measures can be obtained by assessing student performance in a carefully designed test, aimed at pinpointing the achievement of units arranged in a hierarchical sequence. The hierarchy of units represents a set of hypotheses regarding the prerequisites of each capability described. Whether the units do in fact have this hierarchical relation to each other is indicated by the evidence of the test.

The kind of data yielded by the test of these hypotheses can be interpreted to show either that the prerequisite relations are possible ones, or that they represent incorrect arrangements, which do not actually occur that way in a group of instructed students. The data can therefore be used as a basis for a rearrangement of the hierarchy, implying the need for a rearranged sequence of instruction. In such a manner, a curriculum can be designed before it has specifically been used with students.

Following the initial revision, there are of course many additional opportunities to test the appropriateness of a hierarchy underlying a given curriculum. Once the curriculum is used, another attempt can readily be made to measure the achievement of students on each component, using much the same testing technique as before. The second time around provides a considerably more rigorous test, since the instructional sequence has now been more precisely specified. Again, it would not be surprising to find evidence of the need to make additional revisions in the sequence of instruction suggested by the curriculum hierarchy. But the implications of this evidence for revision should in this case be quite clear.

It is often said that curriculum development is a continuous process, rather than a discrete, one-shot affair. Such a statement needs to be taken quite seriously. The method I have described is one which incorporates this idea in an integral fashion. Curriculum design can be, and probably should be, based firmly upon the kind of empirical evidence that can come from successive tryouts and systematic testing. *Any* curriculum can be tested by means of the procedures I have described. Up until very recently, only a few have been.

2. A second kind of implication of these techniques concerns the subject of learning. Most learning studies, even when they are designed around material highly relevant to a school program, have been concerned with determining the effectiveness of learning conditions for *single units* of a curriculum, or at the most, of a very few units. Obviously, the larger problem must be oriented toward the learning, not of a single task, but of an entire sequence of cur-

riculum units. Cronbach (1966), for example, in discussing studies of discovery learning, points out the shortcomings of short sequences of learning tasks in revealing the effectiveness or noneffectiveness of discovery methods of instruction. Similar reasoning may be applied to any method of instruction one wishes to evaluate. We need to have more research studies devoted to an examination of the learning of fairly extended sequences of content, in order to improve our understanding of how students learn.

There are many learning questions to be examined in connection with longer units of instruction. One thinks immediately of investigations of problem-solving strategies, of the timing and frequency of occasions for review, of the processes of knowledge generalization, and many others. It is of importance to note, however, that such studies must solve the problem of specification of the content of curriculum, if they are to yield results of lasting value. One cannot draw valid conclusions about differing *methods* of instruction unless there is an experimental way of controlling *content*. The design of curriculum hierarchies, and the sequences of instruction based upon them, offers one way of solving this difficult methodological problem. If one assesses students' capabilities on these units, a way is provided of matching students. By the same means, one is able to use a standard criterion of learning itself. Possibly the most important implication of curriculum hierarchies for research in learning, therefore, is that they provide a methodology of content control without which the study of extended learning (over a reasonably long sequence of curricular units) is very difficult, if not impossible.

3. But there are additional implications of these techniques for the study of the process of extended-sequence learning. Presumably, more than one hierarchical sequence may end with the same terminal objective, as is true in a gross sense in the addition of integers illustrated in Figure 1. Is one sequence better than another in the sense of producing more rapid or more lasting learning effects?

There is also the whole question of the generalizable effects of a curriculum sequence, in the sense of transfer of learning. It has more than once been pointed out, quite correctly, that the unit capabilities represented in a hierarchy have transfer potentialities that are not indicated in such a diagram. Learning to "supply other names for positive integers in statements of equality," for example, is a capability useful for many other mathematical tasks than that of adding integers — it surely would be expected also to transfer to multiplying and dividing integers, and to the simplifying of other statements of mathematical equality. Similar remarks can be made about the unitary capabilities depicted in Figure 2, on voting behavior. Knowing the functions of the mayor, for example, may be of importance to other kinds of citizenship behavior, such as those of petitioning, maintaining democratic government, effecting change in local government, and a number of others. So we have the whole area of the transfer effects of curriculum units and sequences to study. Are some units more generalizable than others? Do some sequences lead to greater amounts of transfer of learning than others? Again, it is my belief that the method of curriculum development described provides a basic means of studying these questions in a systematic sense, irrespective of the particular content.

4. A related area of research suggested by this method of analysis is that of individual differences or, more specifically, the relation of individual differences to learning. Many speculations have been made regarding the existence of differences of "learning styles," "learning approaches," "learning strategies" among individual learners. Such differences are so evidently and heartily wished for that one almost believes they exist. Yet the fact of the matter seems to be that almost none are verified realities (cf. Gagné, 1966). There has been a rather lengthy history of discouraging research in this general area (Woodrow, 1946).

It seems possible that the method of curriculum development I have described provides some new opportunities for studies designed to relate individual differences to learning variables. Again, it is primarily the possibility of *control* provided by the method which seems of greatest potential significance. As previously mentioned, designing hierarchies of curriculum units makes it possible to specify content in terms of objectives attained at any given point in the process of instruction. Furthermore, it is evident that some important things about the individual student can also be specified or controlled. Two students who have demonstrated their mastery of a curriculum hierarchy up to a given point are in some objective sense exactly alike. Yet we suspect from other evidence that they are also very different. Knowing in what respects they are alike provides an excellent basis for measuring in a highly systematic manner how they differ.

The basic rationale for research on individual differences in learning, under specified conditions of mastery of curriculum units, seems fairly clear. Yet I need to emphasize the warning that in order to study the matter in this way, certain concepts traditional to the field of psychological measurement must be voluntarily abandoned, at least for the purposes of these investigations. The basic measurement to be obtained, and one which provides the means of control, is whether the student *has* or *has not* acquired the specific unitary capability being measured. One cannot admit *degrees* of mastery into this kind of measurement, and one cannot deal with the concept of difficulty. Once such basic measurements are made, one can subsequently ask questions about *other* kinds of individual differences, and presumably these will vary in degree (cf. Gagné, 1965b, pp. 259-263).

The potentialities of this method for getting a new purchase on the problem of individual differences in learning therefore seem quite good. When the learned prerequisites of a task can be specified and controlled within an entire group of learners, fairly precise questions can be formulated about the kinds of differences that may account for such things as rate of learning, permanence of learning effects, or generalizability of learning.

In sum, the method of specifying a curriculum by deriving a hierarchy of capabilities, beginning with educational objectives that describe human performance, seems to have some important implications for research. First, it is a systematic method for designing curricula on the basis of empirical evidence of their feasibility. Such evidence can be obtained initially even before design is undertaken, and can continue to provide corrective inputs to successive stages of the curriculum-development process. In addition, however, it seems evident that this method of specifying content has some useful methodological implications for research on the learning of school subjects. When a learner's capabilities can be measured in terms of mastery of the specified units of a curriculum, a desirable degree of control is attained which then makes possible the study of learning effectiveness under conditions involving experimental variations in timing, sequence, incentive, and other variables. This advantage applies to the study of learning of extended sequences of content having a practical resemblance to those encountered in school situations, and also to the investigation of individual differences in learning.

The Methodology of Evaluation

Michael Scriven[1]

Indiana University

INTRODUCTION

Current conceptions of the evaluation of educational instruments (e.g. new curricula, programmed texts, inductive methods, individual teachers) are still inadequate both philosophically and practically. This paper attempts to exhibit and reduce some of the deficiencies. Intellectual progress is possible only because newcomers can stand on the shoulders of giants. This feat is often confused with treading on their toes, particularly but not only by the newcomer. I confess a special obligation to Professor Cronbach's (1963) work,[2] and to valuable discussions with the personnel of CIRCE at the University of Illinois, as well as thoughtful correspondence from several others, especially James Shaver.

1. OUTLINE

The main focus of this paper is on curricular evaluation but almost all the points made transfer immediately to other kinds of evaluation. Section headings are reasonably self-explanatory and occur in the following order:

1. Outline.
2. Goals of Evaluation versus Roles of Evaluation: Formative and Summative Evaluation.
3. Professional versus Amateur Evaluation.
4. Evaluation Studies versus Process Studies.

[1]An earlier version of this paper was written and circulated during the author's tenure as director of the Evaluation Project of the Social Science Education Consortium, supported by a developmental grant from the U.S. Office of Education, and later by the Kettering Foundation.
[2]In the form of personal comments and correspondence, as well as his well-known article, "Evaluation for Course Improvement," *Teachers' College Record, 64*, No. 8, May, 1963, reprinted in *New Curricula* (R. Heath, Ed., New York: Harper & Row, 1964, pp. 231-248). References in this paper are to the latter version.

The discussion in the earlier sections is relatively elementary and etiological, progressing to an occasionally more difficult and generally more practical level in later sections.

2. GOALS OF EVALUATION VERSUS ROLES OF EVALUATION: FORMATIVE AND SUMMATIVE EVALUATION

The function of evaluation may be thought of in two ways. At the methodological level, we may talk of the *goals* of evaluation; in a particular sociological or pedagogical context we may further distinguish several possible *roles* of evaluation.

In the abstract, we may say that evaluation attempts to answer certain *types of question* about certain *entities*. The entities are the various educational "instruments" (processes, personnel, procedures, programs, etc.). The types of question include questions of the form: *How well* does this instrument perform (with respect to such-and-such criteria)?, Does it perform *better* than this other instrument?, *What* does this instrument do (i.e., what variables from the group in which we are interested are significantly affected by its application)?, Is the use of this instrument *worth* what it's costing? Evaluation is itself a methodological activity which is essentially similar whether we are trying to evaluate coffee machines or teaching machines, plans for a house or plans for a curriculum. The activity consists simply in the gathering and combining of performance data with a weighted set of goal scales to yield either comparative or numerical ratings, and in the justification of (a) the data-gathering instruments, (b) the weightings, and (c) the selection of goals.

But the *role* which evaluation has in a particular educational context may be enormously various; it may form part of a teacher training activity, of the process of curriculum development, of a field experiment connected with the improvement of learning theory, of an investigation preliminary to a decision about purchase or rejection of materials; it may be a data-gathering activity for supporting a request for tax increases or research support, or a preliminary to the reward or punishment of people as in an executive training program, a prison, or a classroom. Failure to make this rather obvious distinction between the roles and goals of evaluation, not necessarily in this terminology, is one of the factors that has led to the dilution of the process of evaluation to the point where it can no longer serve as a basis for answering the questions which are its goal. This dilution has sacrificed goals to roles. One can be against evaluation only if one can show that it is improper to seek an answer to questions about the merit of educational instruments, which would involve showing that there are *no* legitimate activities (roles) in which these questions can be raised, an extraordinary claim. Obviously the fact that evaluation is sometimes given an inappropriate role hardly justifies the conclusion that we *never* need to know the answers to the goal questions. Anxiety about "evaluation," especially among teachers or students, is all too frequently an illicitly generalized response originating in legitimate objections to a situation in which an evaluation was given a role quite beyond its reliability or comprehensiveness.

One role that has often and sensibly been assigned to evaluation is as an important part of the process of curriculum *development* (another is teacher self-improvement). Obviously such a role does not preclude evaluation of the *final* product of this process. Evaluation can and usually should play several roles. But it is clear from the treatment of evaluation in some of the recent literature and in a number of recent research proposals involving several million dollars that the assumption is being made that one's obligations in the direction of evaluation are fully discharged by having it appear *somewhere* in a project. Not only can it have several roles with respect to one educational enterprise, but with respect to each of these it may have several specific goals. Thus, it may have a role in the on-going improvement of the curriculum, and with respect to this role several types of questions (goals) may be raised, such as: Is the curriculum at this point really getting across the distinction between prejudice and commitment?, Is it taking too large a proportion of the available time to make this point?, etc. In another role, the evaluation process may serve to enable administrators to decide whether the entire finished curriculum, refined by use of the evaluation process in its first role, represents a sufficiently significant advance on the available alternatives to justify the expense of adoption by a school system.

One of the reasons for the tolerance or indeed encouragement of the confusion between roles and goals is the well-meaning attempt to allay the anxiety on the part of teachers that the word "evaluation" precipitates. By stressing the constructive part evaluation may play in nonthreatening activities (roles) we slur over the fact that its goals always include the estimation of merit, worth, value, etc., which all too clearly contribute in another role to decisions about promotion and rejection of personnel and courses. But we cannot afford to tackle anxiety about evaluation by ignoring its importance and confusing its presentation; the loss in efficiency is too great. Business firms can't keep executives or factories when they know they are not doing good work and a society shouldn't have to retain textbooks, courses, teachers, and superintendents that do a poor job when a good performance is possible. The appropriate way to handle anxiety of this kind is by finding tasks for which a better prognosis is possible for the individuals whose positions or prestige are threatened. Failure to evaluate pupils' performance leads to the gross inefficiencies of the age-graded classroom or the "ungraded" reports on pupils, and failure to evaluate teachers' performances leads to the correlative inefficiency of incompetent instruction and the substitution of personality for performance. A little toughening of the moral fiber may be required if we are not to shirk the social responsibilities of the educational branch of our culture. Thus, it may even be true that "the greatest service evaluation can perform is to identify aspects of the course where revision is desirable" (Cronbach,[2] p. 236), though it is not clear how one would establish this, but it is certainly also true that there are other extremely important evaluation services which must be done for almost any given curriculum project or other educational innovation. And there are many contexts in which calling in an evaluator to perform a final evaluation of the project or person is an act of proper recognition of responsibility to the person, product, or taxpayers. It therefore seems a little excessive to refer to this as simply "a menial role," as Cronbach does. It is obviously a great service if this kind of terminal, overall, or "outcome" evaluation can demonstrate that a very expensive textbook (etc.) is not significantly better than the competition, or that it is enormously better than any competitor. In more general terms it may be possible to demonstrate that a certain type of approach to (for example) mathematics is not yielding significantly better pupil performance on any dimension that mathematicians or vocational users are prepared to regard as important. This would certainly save a great deal of expenditure of time and money and constitute a valuable contribution to educational development, as would the converse, favorable, result. Thus there seem to be a number of qualifications that would have to be made before one could accept a statement asserting the greater importance of formative evaluation by comparison with summative. ("Evaluation, used to improve the course while it is still fluid, contributes more to improvement of education than evaluation used to appraise a product already placed on the market."—Cronbach,[2] p. 236) Fortunately we do not have to make this choice. Educational projects, particularly curricular ones, clearly must attempt to make best use of evaluation in both these roles. As a matter of terminology, I think that novel terms are worthwhile here, to avoid inappropriate connotations, and I propose to use the terms "formative" and "summative" to qualify evaluation in these roles.

process
r/t
outcome

Now any curriculum builder is almost automatically engaged in formative evaluation, except on a very strict interpretation of "evaluation." He is presumably doing what he is doing because he judges that the material being presented in the existing curriculum is unsatisfactory. So, as he proceeds to construct the new material, he is constantly evaluating his own material as better than that which is already current. Unless entirely ignorant of one's shortcomings as a judge of one's own work, he is also presumably engaged in field-testing the work while it is being developed, and in so doing he gets feedback on the basis of which he again produces revisions; this is of course formative evaluation. If the field-testing is elaborate, it may amount to summative evaluation of *the early forms* of the new curriculum. He is usually involved with colleagues, e.g. the classroom teacher or peers, who comment on the material as they see it—again, this is evaluation, and it produces changes which are allegedly for the better.

If a recommendation for formative evaluation has any content at all, it presumably amounts to the suggestion that a *professional* evaluator should be added to the curriculum construction project. There certainly can be advantages in this, though it is equally clear from practical experience that there can be disadvantages. But this question is clearly not the same as the question whether to have summative evaluation. We devote part of the next section to a discussion of these two questions.

3. PROFESSIONAL VERSUS AMATEUR EVALUATION

The basic fact is that the evaluator, while a professional in his own field, is usually not a professional in the field relevant to the curriculum being reformed or, if he is, he is not committed to the particular development being undertaken. This leads to clashes and counter-charges of a kind which are all too familiar to project directors today.

From these "failures of communication" between evaluators and teachers or curriculum makers there have sprung some unfortunate overreactions. The hard-nosed anti-evaluation line is all too frequently a rationalization of the anxiety provoked by the presence of an external judge who is not identified with or committed to (or perhaps does not even understand) the ideals of the project. The equally indefensible opposite extreme is represented by the self-perceived tough-minded operationalist evaluator, all too likely to say "If you can't tell me what variables you claim to be affecting, in operational terms, we can't construct a test for their variation, and as long as they haven't been tested you haven't any reason for thinking you are making a contribution."

In order to develop a fair treatment of these views let us consider the difference between a contemporary educational project involving the development of a new curriculum or teaching method, and the co-authoring of a new ninth-grade algebra text by two or three teachers in the late 1930's. In the first place, the present projects are often supported from government funds on a very large scale. The justification of this expenditure calls for some kind of objective evidence that the product is valuable. Moreover *future* support for work in this area or by these same workers requires some objective evidence as to their merit at this kind of job. Since there are not sufficient funds to support all applicants, judgments of comparative merit are necessary; and objective bases for this are obviously superior to mere person-endorsements by peers, etc. Finally, the enormous costs involved in the *adoption* of such products by school systems commit another great slice of taxpayers' money, and this kind of commitment should presumably be made only on the basis of rather substantial evidence for its justification. In this context, summative evaluation is an inescapable obligation on the project director, an obvious requirement by the sponsoring agency, and a desideratum as far as the schools are concerned. And since formative evaluation is a necessary part of any rational approach to producing good results on the summative evaluation, it can hardly be wholly eschewed; indeed, as we have shown, its occurrence is to some degree guaranteed by the nature of the case. But the separate question of whether and how professional evaluators should be employed depends very much upon the extent to which they do more harm than good—and there are a number of ways in which they can do harm.

Professional evaluators may simply exude a kind of skeptical spirit that dampens the creative fires of a productive group. They may be sympathetic but impose such crushing demands on operational formulation of goals as to divert too much time to an essentially secondary activity. ("Secondary" in the sense that there cannot be any evaluation without a curriculum.) The major compromise that must be effected is to have the evaluator recognize it as partly *his* responsibility to uncover and formulate a testable set of criteria for the course. He may be substantially helped by the fact that the project has explicitly espoused certain goals, or rejected others, and he will certainly be aided by the writing team's criticism of his formulations. However, the exchange has to be a two-way one; curriculum writers are by no means infallible, and often are extremely prejudiced or grandiose in describing their operations. Evaluators, on the other hand, are handicapped so long as they are less than fully familiar with the subject matter being restructured, and less than fully sympathetic with the aims of the creative group. Yet once they become identified with those aims, emotionally as well as economically, they lose something of great importance to an objective evaluation—their independence. For this reason the formative evaluators should, if at all possible, be sharply distinguished from the summative evaluators, with whom they may certainly work in developing an acceptable summative evaluation schema, but the formative evaluators should ideally exclude themselves from the role of judge in the summative evaluation. If this distinction between formative and summative evaluation personnel is made, it becomes possible to retain the advantages of eventual objective professional evaluation without the risks of disrupting the team spirit during development.

There are other problems about the intrusion of evaluation into education, and the intrusion of an evaluator into the curriculum-making process. Several of these have been admirably expressed by J. Myron Atkin (1963). Some of them are taken up elsewhere in this paper, but some mention of two of them should be made here. The first suggestion is that testing for the extent of learning of certain rather delicate and pervasive concepts may be itself destructive, in that it makes the student too self-conscious about the role of a concept at too early a stage, thereby preventing its natural and proper development. The problem is that with respect to some of these concepts, e.g. symmetry, equilibrium, and randomness, it might be the case that very little accretion occurs in the understanding of a child during any particular course or indeed any particular year of his education, but that tiny accretion may be of very great importance in the long-run development of good scientific understanding. It would not show up on tests, indeed it might be stultified by the intrusion of tests, in any given year, but it has to be in the curriculum in order to produce the finished product that we desire. In this case, evaluation seems to be both incompetent and possibly destructive.

Such a possibility should serve as an interesting challenge to the creative curriculum-maker. While not dismissing it, he would normally respond by attempting to treat it more explicitly, perhaps at a somewhat later stage in the curriculum than it is normally first mentioned, and see whether some significant and satisfactory accretion of comprehension cannot be produced by this direct attack. Only if this failed would he turn to the evaluator and demand a considerably more sensitive instrument. Again, it would also be possible to deliberately avoid testing for this during all the early years of its peripheral introduction, and test only in the senior year in high school, for example. We can acknowledge the *possibility* that concerns Atkin and allow some extra material in the curriculum to handle it even without any justification in the early feedback from tests. Errors of excess are much less significant than errors of commission or omission in curriculum-making.

It is well known that there are dangers from having a curriculum-making group discuss its work with teachers of the present curriculum — although there are obviously possible advantages from this — so there are dangers and advantages in bringing the evaluator in early. In such situations, some ingenuity on the part of the project director will often make the best of both worlds possible; for example, the evaluator may be simply introduced to the materials produced, but not to the people producing them, and his comments studied by the director with an eye to feeding back any fundamental and serious criticisms, but withholding the others until some later stage in the curriculum development activities where, for example, an extensive process of revision is about to begin. But these are practical considerations; there remain two more fundamental kinds of objection that should be mentioned briefly, of which the first is central to Atkin's misgivings.

No one who has been involved in the field-testing of a new curriculum has failed to notice the enormous variability in its appeal to students, often unpredictable from their previous academic performance. The child already interested in bird-watching may find one approach to biology far more attractive than another. Similarly, for some children the relevance of the material to problems with which they are familiar will make an enormous difference to their interest, whereas for others the properties of those curious entities the hexaflexagons and the Moebius strips are immediately fascinating. More fundamentally, the structuring of the classroom situation may wholly alter the motivation for different students in different ways; the nondirective style of treatment currently regarded as desirable, partly for its supposed connection with the inductive approach, is totally unstimulating for some children, although an aggressive, competitive, critical interaction will get them up and running. In the face of this kind of variation, we are often committed to the use of the very blunt evaluation instrument of the performance, on tests, of the class as a whole. Even if we break this down into improvements in individual performances, we still have not fully exploited the potentialities of the material, which would be manifested only if we were to select the right material *and* the right instructional technique for a child with a particular background, attitudes, interests, and abilities. Perhaps, the antievaluation skeptic suggests, it is more appropriate to place one's faith in the creative and academically impeccable curriculum maker, using the field tests simply to make sure that it is *possible* to excite and teach students with the material, under appropriate circumstances. That is, our criterion should be markedly improved performance by *some,* even by a *substantial* number, rather than by the class as a whole. To this the evaluator must reply by asking whether one is to disregard possibilities such as serious lack of comprehensibility to many students at this age-level, a marked relative deterioration of performance in some of the students more than offsetting the gains in others, the possibility that it is the pedagogical skill or enthusiasm of the teacher that is responsible for the success in the field tests and not the materials. The material is to go out to other teachers; it must be determined whether it will be of any use to them. To answer these questions — and indeed for the field tests themselves — a professional job in evaluation is necessary.

We can learn something important from this criticism, however. We must certainly weigh seriously the opinions of the subject matter expert as to the flavor and quality of the curriculum content. Sometimes it will be almost all we have to go on, and sometimes it will even be enough for some decisions. It should in any event be seriously considered and sometimes heavily weighted in the evaluation process, for the *absence* of supporting professional consensus of this kind is often adequate grounds for complete rejection of the material.

Finally, there is the objection that hovers in the background of many of these discussions, the uneasy feeling that evaluation necessitates making value judgments and that value judgments are essentially subjective and not scientific. This is about as intelligent a view as the view that statements about oneself are essentially subjective and hence incapable of rational substantiation. Some value judgments are essentially assertions about fundamental personal preferences ("matters of taste") and as such are factual claims which can be established or refuted by ordinary (though sometimes not easy) procedures of psychological investigation. The process of establishing this kind of claim does not show that it is right or wrong for everyone to hold these values; it only shows that it is true that somebody does or does not hold them. Another kind of value judgment is the assessment of the merit or comparative merit of some entity in a clearly defined context where this amounts to a claim that its performance is as good as or better than another's on clearly identifiable and clearly weighted criterion variables. With respect to value judgments of this kind, it is not only possible to find out whether or not they are believed by the individuals who assert them, but it is also possible to determine whether it is right or wrong for anyone to believe them. They are simply complex conflations of various performance ratings and the weightings of the various performances; it is in this sense that we can correctly assert that the Bulova Accutron is the best wrist chronometer currently available or that a particular desk dictionary is the best one for somebody with extensive scientific interests. Finally, there are value judgments in which the criteria themselves are debatable, a type of value judgment which is only philosophically the most important and whose debatability merely reflects the fact that important issues are not always easy ones. Examples of this would be the assertion that the most important role of evaluation is in the process of curriculum writing, or that the IQ test is an unfortunate archaism, or that the Copenhagen interpretation of quantum physics is superior to any known alternative. In each of these cases, the disputes turn out to be mainly disputes about what is to count as good, rather than to be arguments about the straightforward "facts of the situation," i.e., what is in fact good. It is immature to react to this kind of judgment as if it is contaminated with some disgusting disease; the only proper reaction is to examine the reasons that are put forward for them and see if and how the matter

may be rationally discussed. The history of the greatest develop-
ments in science is the history of the rational triumph of such value
judgments, of new conceptions of "good explanation," "good
theory," "good model" ("paradigm"), not just of one theory over
another in a contest where the rules are agreed.

It is sometimes thought that in dealing with people, as we must
in the field of education, we are necessarily involved in the field of
moral value judgments, and that at least *these* really are essentially
subjective. But in the first place value judgments about people are
by no means necessarily moral, since they may refer to their health,
intelligence, and achievements; secondly, even if they are moral,
we are all presumably committed to one moral principle (the principle of the equality of rights of men) and by far the greater part of
public moral discourse depends only on the framework built on this
assumption with complicated empirical judgments about the consequences of alternatives.[3] So, unless one is willing to challenge
this axiom, and to provide rational support for an alternative, even
moral value judgments are within the realm of rational debate. But
whatever the outcome of such a discussion, the facts that some
evaluation is moral evaluation and that some moral evaluation is
controversial do not conjointly imply the least degree of support
for the conclusion that curricular evaluation is less than a fully
appropriate goal for applied science.

4. EVALUATION STUDIES VERSUS
PROCESS STUDIES

In the course of clarifying the concept of evaluation it is important not to simplify it. Although the *typical* goals of evaluation
require judgments of merit and worth, when somebody is asked to
evaluate a situation or the impact of certain kinds of materials on
the market, then what is being called for is an analytical description of the process, usually with respect to certain possible causal
connections, indeed an *interpretation* (see Section 13 below). In
this sense it is not inappropriate to regard some kinds of process
investigation as evaluation. But the range of process research only
overlaps with and is neither subsumed by nor equivalent to that of
evaluation. We may conveniently distinguish three types of process
research, as the term is used by Cronbach and others.

1. The noninferential study of what actually goes on in the class-

---

[3]Discussed in more detail by the author in, e.g., "Morality" in *Primary Philosophy*
(New York: McGraw-Hill, 1966).

room. Perhaps this has the most direct claim to being called a study of the process of teaching (learning, etc.). We might for example be interested in the proportion of the class period during which the teacher talks, the amount of time that the students spend in homework for a class, the proportion of the dialogue devoted to explaining, defining, opining, etc. (Milton Meux and B. O. Smith, 1961). The great problem about work like this is to show that it is worth doing, in *any* sense. *Some* pure research is idle research. The Smith and Meux work is specifically mentioned because *it* is clearly original and offers promise in a large number of directions. Skinner's attack on controlled studies and his emphasis on process research are more than offset by his social-welfare orientation which ensures that the process work is aimed at valuable improvements in control of learning. It is difficult to avoid the conclusion, however, that most process research of this kind in education, as in psychotherapy (though apparently not in medicine), is fruitful at neither the theoretical nor the applied level.

2. The second kind of process research involves the investigation of causal claims ("dynamic hypotheses") about the process. Here we are interested in such questions as whether an increase of time spent on class discussions of the goals of a curriculum at the expense of time spent on training drills leads to improved comprehension in (a) algebra, (b) geography, etc. This kind of investigation is essentially a miniature limited-scope "new instrument" project. Another kind looks for the answer to such questions as: Is the formation of subgroup allegiance and identification with the teacher facilitated by strong emphasis on pupil-teacher dialogue? The feature of this subgroup of process hypotheses that distinguishes them from evaluation hypotheses is that the dependent variables either are ones which would not figure among the set of criteria we would use in a summative evaluation study (though we might think of them as important because of their relevance to improved teaching techniques) or they are only a subgroup of such summative criteria; and in either case no attempt is made to justify any correlative assignments of merit.

Process hypotheses of this second kind are in general about as difficult to substantiate as any "outcome" hypothesis, i.e., summative evaluation. Indeed they are sometimes harder to substantiate because they may require identifying the effects of only one of several independent variables that are present, and it is extremely hard – though usually not impossible – to apply ordinary matching techniques to take care of the others. The advantage of some summative evaluation investigation is that it is concerned with evaluating the effects of a whole teacher-curriculum package and has no need to identify the specific agent responsible for the overall improvement or deterioration. That advantage lapses when we are concerned to identify the variance due to the curriculum as opposed to the teacher.

3. Formative Evaluation. This kind of research is often called process research, but it is of course simply outcome evaluation of an intermediate stage in the development of the teaching instrument. The distinction between this and the first kind of dynamic hypothesis mentioned above is twofold. There is a distinction of role: the role of formative evaluation is to discover deficiencies and successes in the intermediate versions of a new curriculum; the role of dynamic hypothesis investigation is *sui generis:* it is to provide the answer to an important question about the mechanism of teaching. And there is a distinction in the extent to which it matters whether the criteria used are an adequate analysis of the proper goals of the curriculum. The dynamic hypothesis study has no obligation to this; the formative evaluation does. But the two types of study are not always sharply distinct. They both play an important role in good curriculum research.

Now of course it is true that anybody who does an experiment of any kind at all should at some stage evaluate *his results.* It is even true that the experiment itself will usually be designed in such a way as to incorporate procedures for evaluation of the results – e.g. by using an "objectively validated" test, which has a certain kind of built-in comparative evaluation in the scoring key. None of this shows that most research is evaluation research. In particular, even process research is not all evaluation research. That interpretation of data can be described as evaluation of results does not show that the interpretations (and the explanations) are about the *merit* of a teaching instrument. They may, for example, be about the temporal duration of various elements of the instrument, etc. Such points are obvious enough, but a good deal of the comment pro and con evaluation research betokens considerable lack of clarity about its boundaries.

5. EVALUATION VERSUS ESTIMATION OF GOAL ACHIEVEMENT

One of the reactions to the threat of evaluation, or perhaps to the use of over-crude evaluative procedures, was the extreme relativization of evaluation research. The slogan became: How well does the course achieve its goals? instead of How good is the course? but it is obvious that if the goals aren't worth achieving then it is uninteresting how well they are achieved. The success of this kind of relativism in the evaluation field rests entirely upon the premise that judgments of goals are subjective value judgments not open to rational argument. No doubt they often are; but this in no way indicates that the field is one in which objectivity is impossible. An American History curriculum, K-14, which consisted in the memorization of names and dates would be absurd—it could not possibly be said to be a good curriculum, no matter how well it attained its goals. Nor could one which led to absolutely no recall of names or chronology. A "Modern Math" curriculum for general use which produced high school graduates largely incapable of reliable addition and multiplication would be (and possibly is) simply a disgrace, no matter what else it conveyed. This kind of value judgment about goals is not beyond debate, but *good* arguments to the contrary have not been forthcoming so far. These are value judgments with excellent backing. Nor is their defensibility due to their lack of specificity. Much more precise ones can be given just as excellent backing; a physics curriculum which does not discuss the kinetic theory at any stage would be deficient, no matter how well it achieved whatever goals it had. And so on.

Thus evaluation proper must include, as an equal partner with the measuring of performance against goals, procedures for the evaluation of the goals. That is, if it is to have any reference to goals at all. In the next two sections we will discuss procedures of evaluation that involve reference to goals and procedures which attempt to short-circuit such reference. First it should be pointed out that it is one thing to maintain that judgment of goals is part of evaluation, i.e., that we cannot just accept anyone's goals, and quite another to maintain that these goals should be the same for every school, for every school district, for every teacher, for every level, etc. It is entirely appropriate that a school with primarily vocational responsibilities should have somewhat different goals from those of a school producing 95 per cent college-bound graduates. It just does not follow from this that the people who give the course or run the school or design the curriculum can be regarded as in any way immune from criticism in setting up their goals. A great deal of the energy behind the current attempts to reform the school curriculum springs straight out of the belief that the goals have been fundamentally wrong, that life-adjustment has been grossly overweighted, etc. To swing in the opposite direction is all too easy, and in no way preferable.

The process of relativization, however, has not only led to over-tolerance for over-restrictive goals, but has also led to incompetent evaluation of the extent to which these are achieved. Whatever one's views about evaluation, it is easy enough to demonstrate that there are very few professionally competent evaluators in the country today. The United States Office of Education's plans for Research and Development centers, relatively modest in terms of the need, will certainly be unfulfillable because of the staffing problem as far as their evaluation commitments are concerned. The heavily financed curriculum projects already in existence are themselves badly understaffed on the evaluation side, even on the most conservative view of its role. The staff are themselves often well aware of their limitations, and in-service training projects for them are badly needed. The very idea that every school system, or every teacher, can today be regarded as capable of meaningful evaluation of his own performance is as absurd as the view that every psychotherapist today is capable of evaluating his work with his own patients. Trivially, they can learn something very important from carefully studying their own work; indeed they can identify some good and bad features about it. But if they or someone else need to know the answers to the important questions, whether process or outcome, they need skills and resources which are conspicuous by their rarity even at the *national* level.

6. "INTRINSIC" EVALUATION VERSUS "PAY-OFF" EVALUATION

Two basically different approaches to the evaluation of a teaching instrument appear possible, and are often contrasted in the literature. If you want to evaluate a tool, say an axe, you might study the design of the bit, the weight distribution, the steel alloy used, the grade of hickory in the handle, etc., or you might just study the kind and speed of the cuts it makes in the hands of a good axeman. (In either case, the evaluation may be either summative or formative, for these are roles of evaluation, not procedures for doing evaluation.)

The first approach involves an appraisal of the instrument itself; in the analog this would involve evaluation of the content, goals, grading procedures, teacher attitude, etc. We shall call this kind of approach intrinsic evaluation. The criteria are usually not operationally formulated, and they refer to the instrument itself. The second approach proceeds via an examination of the effects of the teaching instrument on the pupil, and these alone, and it usually specifies these rather operationally. It involves an appraisal of the differences between pre- and post-tests, between experimental group tests and control group tests, etc., on a number of criterial parameters. We can call this pay-off evaluation. Defenders of the second procedure would support their approach by arguing that all that really counts are the effects of the course on the pupils, appeal to the evaluation of goals and content being defensible only insofar as evaluations of these really correlate with pay-off evaluations. Since these correlations are largely a priori in our present state of knowledge, they argue, the intrinsic approach is too much an armchair affair. The intrinsic evaluator is likely to counter by talking about important values that do not show up in the outcome study to which the pay-off man restricts himself, due to the deficiencies of present test instruments and scoring procedures: he is likely to exemplify this claim by reference to qualities of a curriculum such as elegance, modernity, structure, integrity, readiness considerations, etc., which can best be judged by looking at the materials directly.

The possibility obviously emerges that an evaluation involving some weighting of intrinsic criteria and some of pay-off criteria might be a worthwhile compromise. There are certain kinds of evaluation situation where this will be so, but before any assessment of the correct relative weighting is possible it is necessary to look a little further into the nature of the two pure alternatives.

It was maintained in the preceding section that evaluation in terms of goal achievement is typically a very poor substitute for good summative evaluation, since it merely relativizes the problem. If we are going to evaluate in a way that brings in goals at all, then we shall typically have some obligation to evaluate the goals. The trouble with "intrinsic" evaluation is that it brings in what might be called intermediate goals or criteria, and hence automatically raises the question of the value of these criteria, presumably by reference to the pay-off criteria. One of the charms of the pay-off type of evaluation is the lack of charm, indeed the messiness, of a thorough intrinsic evaluation.

A major difficulty with evaluation involving intermediate goals, which is the key feature of an "intrinsic" approach, lies in the *formulation* of the goals. In the first place the verbally espoused goals of a curriculum-maker are often not the implicit goals of his curriculum. Moreover, it is not always the case that this kind of error should be corrected in favor of the espoused goals by revising the curriculum or in favor of the implicit goals by revising the espoused goals. How do we decide which should receive prece-

dence? Even if we were able to decide this, there is the perennial
headache of translating the description of the goals that we get
from the curriculum-maker or the curriculum-analyst into testable
terms. Many a slip occurs between that lip and the cup.

In addition to this, there is the problem already mentioned, that
putting pressure on a writer to formulate his goals, to keep to
them, and to express them in testable terms may enormously alter
his product in ways that are certainly not always desirable. Perhaps
the best way of handling this third problem is to give prospective
curriculum-builders an intensive short course in evaluation techniques and problems prior to their commencing work. Such a
course would be topic-neutral, and would thereby avoid the
problems of criticism of one's own "baby." Interaction with a
professional evaluator can then be postponed substantially and
should also be less anxiety-provoking. Short courses of the kind
mentioned should surely be available for subsidized attendance
every summer at one or two centers in the country. Ignoring any
further consideration of the problem of in-group harmony, and this
proposal for improving formative evaluation, we can turn to the
practical problem of evaluation.

7. PRACTICAL SUGGESTIONS FOR MEDIATED EVALUATION

Any curriculum project has some kind of general objectives at the
very beginning. Even if these are only put in terms of producing a
more interesting or more up-to-date treatment, there must be some
kind of grounds for dissatisfaction with the present curriculum if
the project is to be a worthwhile activity. Usually something rather
more specific emerges in the course of planning discussions. For
example, the idea of a three-track approach, aimed at various kinds
of teacher or student interest, may emerge out of a rather explicit
discussion of the aims of a project, when it becomes clear that three
equally defensible aims can be formulated which will lead to
incompatible requirements for the curriculum. Or, which amounts
to the same, the same aim — in a very general sense — can be served
in three equally defensible ways. These "ways" then become
intermediate goals to be served by the curriculum. The mere fact
that these aims can be seen as incompatible makes clear that they
must have fairly substantial content. Another typical content
presupposition refers to coverage; it is recognized from the beginning that at least certain topics should be covered, or if they are not

then there must be some compensatory coverage of other topics. Typically, a project involves at least some of these abstractly formulated goals, and we shall call such studies "mediated." This is not quite the same as a pure intrinsic evaluation, because it may involve *some* pay-off criteria.

At this early stage of discussing the curriculum a member or members of the project team should be appointed to the task of goal-formulation. Many of the objections to this kind of activity stem from reactions to over-rigid requirements for the way in which goals can be formulated at this stage. Any kind of goal on which the group agrees, however abstractly or specifically formulated, even goals which it agrees should be considered as a possibility in the developing stage, should be listed at this point. None of them should be regarded as absolute commitments in any way — simply as reminders. It is not possible to overlook the unfortunate examples of projects in which the creative urge has outdistanced reality restraints; it has to be faced from the beginning that too gross a divergence from a certain minimum coverage is going to make the problem of adoption insuperable. If adoption is a goal, it should be listed along with the motivational and cognitive ones. Having market-type goals such as substantial adoption on the list is in no way inappropriate: one can hardly reform education with curricula that never reach the classroom. But one may think it desirable at an early stage (if it is possible) to translate such goals into constraints on content, e.g. on coverage, vocabulary, and attitudes towards society's sacred cows, etc.

As the project develops, three types of activities centering around the formulation of goals should be distinguished and encouraged. In the first place the goals as so far formulated should be regularly reexamined and modified in the light of divergences from them that have arisen during the developmental activities, where it is felt that these changes have led to other, more valuable goals. Even if no modification seems appropriate, the reexamination serves the useful purpose of reminding the writers of overall goals.

Secondly, work should be begun on the construction of a test-question pool. Progress tests will be given, and the items in these can be thrown into this pool. The construction of this pool is the construction of the operational version of the goals. It should therefore be scrutinized at the same time as reexamination of the more abstractly formulated goals occurs. Even though the project is only at the stage of finishing the first unit of a projected ten-unit curriculum, it is entirely appropriate to be formulating questions of the kind that it is proposed to include in the final examination on the final unit or, for that matter, in a follow-up quiz a year later. It is a commonplace that in the light of formulating such questions, the conception of the goals of the course will be altered. It is undesirable to devote a large proportion of the time to this activity, but it is typically not "undue influence" to encourage thinking about course goals in terms of "What kind of question would tap this learning achievement or motivation change in the final examination or in a follow-up test?" At times the answer to this will rightly be "None at all!" because not all values in a course manifest themselves in the final or later examinations. But where they do *not* thereby manifest themselves, some indication should be given of the time and manner in which they might be expected to be detectable; as in career choices, adult attitudes, etc.

The third activity that should commence at an intermediate stage in curriculum development is that of getting some external judgments as to the cohesiveness of the alleged goals, the actual content, and the test question pool. Without this, the validity of the tests and/or the utility of the curriculum will suffer, possibly fatally. There is no need at all for the individual judge at this task to be a professional evaluator; indeed professional evaluators are frequently extremely bad at this. A good logician, a historian of science, a professional in the subject-matter field, an educational psychologist, or a curriculum expert are possible resource categories. The necessary skill, a very striking one when located, is not co-extensive with any standard professional requirement; we might call it "consistency analysis." This is an area where appointments should not be made without trial periods. It is worth considering whether the activities of this individual, at least in a trial period, may be best conducted without face-to-face confrontation with the project team. A brief written report may be adequate to indicate the extent of possible useful information from this source at this stage. But at some stage, and the earlier the better, this kind of activity is essential if gross divergences between (a) espoused, (b) implicit, and (c) tested-for goals are to be avoided. Not only can a good consistency analyst prevent sidetracking of the project by runaway creative fervor, misconceptions of its actual achievement, etc., but he can provide a valuable stimulus to new lines of development. He must be alert for deficiencies in the item-pool as well as superfluities, for omissions in the general list of goals as well as irrelevancies. Ultimately, the justification of psychotherapy does not lie in the fact that the therapist *felt* he was doing the patient some good, but in the fact that he was; and the same applies to curricular research.

If the above procedure is followed throughout the development of a curriculum, we will end up with an oversize question pool of which one should be prepared to say that any significant desired outcome of the course will show up on the answers to these questions and that what does show up will (normally) only come from the course. Possession of this pool has various important advantages. In the first and second place, it is an operational encapsulation of the goals of the course (if the various cross-checks on its construction have been adequate) which can be used (i) to give the students an idea of what is expected of them as well as (ii) to provide a pool from which the final examinations can be constructed. In the third place it can be used by the curriculum-developer to get an extremely detailed picture of his own success (and the success of the cross-checks on pool construction) by administering a different random sample of questions from this pool to each student in a formative evaluation study, instead of administering a given random sample to every student as justice perhaps requires in a final examination.[4]

What has been described is the bare bones of an adequate mediated evaluation. We have made some reference to content characteristics as one of the types of goal, because curriculum groups frequently argue that one of the merits of their output is its superiority as a representation of contemporary advanced thinking about the subject. The natural way to test this is to have the course read through by some highly qualified experts in the field. It is obvious that special difficulties arise over this procedure. For the most that we can learn from it is that the course does not contain any gross distortions of the best contemporary views, or gross deficiencies with respect to them. There remains the question, as the pay-off evaluator would be the first to point out, of the extent to which the material is being communicated. Even a course with gross oversimplifications, professionally repugnant though it may be to the academic expert, may be getting across a better idea of the truth about its subject than a highbrow competitor. The real advantage of the preceding methodology is to provide a means for jumping the gap between intrinsic and pay-off evaluation, between mere measures of goal-achievement and complete evaluation.

A number of further refinements on the above outline are extremely desirable, and necessary in any serious study. They center around the role of the consistency analysis, and they are crucial for formative evaluation studies, rather than summative, since they

---

[4]See Cronbach, p. 242.

help diagnose the cause of poor results. Essentially, we need to know about the success of three connected matching problems: first, the match between goals and course content; second, the match between goals and examination content; third, the match between course content and examination content. Technically we only need to determine two of these in order to be able to evaluate the third; but in fact there are great advantages in attempting to get an estimate of each independently, in order to reduce the error range. We have talked as if one person or group might make each of these matching estimates. It is clearly most desirable that they should all be done independently, and in fact duplicated by independent workers. Only in this way are we likely to be able to track down the real source of disappointing results. Even the P.S.S.C. study, which has been as thoroughly tested as most recent curriculum projects, has nowhere approached the desirable level of analysis indicated here.

In general, of course, the most difficult problem in tests and measurement theory is the problem of construct validity, and the present problem is essentially an exercise in construct validity. The problem can be ignored only by someone who is prepared to accept immediately the consequence that their supposed goals cannot be regarded as met by the course, or that their examinations do not test what the course teaches, or that the examinations do not test the values/materials that are supposed to be imparted by the course. There are, in practice, many ways in which one can implement the need for the comparisons here described; the use of Q-sorts and R-sorts, matching and projective tests for the analysis, etc. In one way or another the job has to be done, if we are going to do a mediated evaluation at all, i.e., if we are going to bring in goals described in any way except by simply giving the questions to be asked on the final examination.

8. THE POSSIBILITY OF PURE PAY-OFF EVALUATION

The operationalist in this area, the "pay-off" evaluator, watches the developing intricacies of the above kind of experimental design with scorn, for he believes that the whole idea of bringing in goal- or content-assessment is not only an irrelevant but also an extremely unreliable procedure for doing the job of course evaluation. In his view it isn't very important to examine what a teacher says he is doing, or what the students say he is doing (or they are learning), or even what the teacher says in class and the students read in the texts; the only important datum is what the student says (does, believes, etc.) at the end of the course that he wouldn't have said at the beginning (or, to be more precise, would not have said at the end if he had not taken this course). In short, says the hard-headed one, let's just see what the course does, and let's not bother with the question of whether it had good intentions.

But the operationalist has difficulties of his own. He cannot avoid the construct validity issue entirely, that is, he cannot avoid the enormous difficulties involved in correctly describing *at a useful level of generality* what the student has learned. It is easy enough to give the exact results of the testing in terms of the percentage of the students who gave certain answers to each specific question; but what we need to know is whether we can say, in the light of their answers, that they have a *better* understanding of the elements of astronomy, or the chemical-bond approach to chemistry, or the ecological approach to biology. And it is a long way from data about answers to specific questions, to that kind of conclusion. It is not necessary for the route to lie through a discussion of abstract, intermediate goals—the operationalist is quite right about this. But *if* it does not lie through a discussion of goals, then we shall not have available the data that we need (a) to distinguish between importantly different explanations of success or failure, (b) to give reasons for using the new text or curriculum to those whose explicit aim *is* the provision of better understanding of the chemical-bond approach. And the latter really *is* a responsibility of the evaluator. For an example of (a), if we attempt a pure pay-off approach to evaluating a curriculum, and discover that the material retained and/or regurgitated by the student is regarded as grossly inadequate by the subject-matter specialists, we have no idea whether this is due to an inadequacy in the intentions of the curriculum-makers, or to imperfections in their curriculum with respect to these goals, or to deficiencies in their examinations with respect to either of the preceding. And thus we cannot institute a remedial program—our only recourse is to start all over. The pay-off approach can be very costly.

To illustrate (b): Suppose that we try a pure pay-off approach and have the students' performance at the end of the course, and only this, rated by an external judge. Who do we pick for a judge? The answer to that question appears to depend on our commitment on our own part to certain intermediate goals which we might as well have acknowledged explicitly. The evaluator will have to relate the students' performance to *some* abstract criterion, whether it is his conception of an adequate professional comprehension, or

what he thinks it is reasonable to expect a tenth-grader to understand, or what somebody should understand who will not continue
to college, etc. The operationalist is right in saying that we can
dispense with any discussion of goals and still discover exactly
what students have learned, and right to believe that the latter is
the most important variable; but he is mistaken if he supposes
that we can in general give the kind of description of what is
learned that is valuable for our purposes, or give a justification for
the curriculum without any reference to abstract goals. At some
stage, someone is going to have to decide what performances count
as adequate comprehension for students at a particular level, for a
particular subject, and then apply this decision to the data about
the students' subsequent behavior, in order to come up with the
overall evaluation. So the operationalism of pay-off evaluation is
somewhat superficial. At this stage of the debate between the
supporter of pure pay-off and that of mediated evaluation, the latter
would seem to be having the best of it.

But the issue is not so one-sided; the operationalist is performing
an invaluable service in reminding us of the potential irresponsi-
bility of producing "elegant," "up-to-date," "rigorous" curricula
if these qualities are not coming through to the students. We can
take them on faith insofar as they are recognized as being the
frosting on the cake, but we can't take the food-value of the cake on
faith. The only real alternative which the operationalist position
leads to is the use of an academic evaluator who is asked to look,
not at the curriculum materials nor the test-item pool, but at the
exact performance of the class on each question, and from this
directly assess the adequacy of the course to the subject as he sees
it. Of course, we still suffer with respect to diagnosing the cause
of deficiencies and hence this is poor formative methodology; but
we can simplify summative evaluation by this device.

So we must add to our comprehensive design a thorough analysis
of the *results* of the students' tests, and not only of the course and
examination content. It is not adequate to go to great trouble setting
up and cross-analyzing the goals, tests, and content of a curriculum
and then attempt to use a percentage-of-possible-maximum-points
figure as the indication of goal achievement (unless the figure
happens to be pretty close to 100 per cent or 0 per cent). This kind
of gross approach is no longer acceptable as evaluation. The
performance of the students on the final tests, as upon the tests at
intermediate stages, must be analyzed in order to determine the
exact locations of shortcomings of comprehension, shortages of
essential facts, lack of practice in basic skills, etc. Percentages are

not very important. It is the *nature* of the mistakes that is important in evaluating the curriculum, and in rewriting it. The technique of the large question pool provides us with an extremely refined instrument for locating deficiencies in the curriculum. But this instrument can only be exploited fully if evaluation of the results is itself handled in a refined way, with the same use of independent judges, hypothesis formation and testing about the nature of the mistakes, longitudinal analysis of same-student variations, etc. It should be clear that the task of proper evaluation of curriculum materials is an enormous one. The use of essay type questions, the development and use of novel instruments, the use of reports by laboratory-work supervisors, the colligation of all this material into specially developed rating schemata, all of this is expensive and time-consuming. It is not more time-consuming than good R & D work in engineering, however. In a later section some comment will be made on the consequences of this conception of the scale of evaluation activities. At this point, however, it becomes necessary to look into a further and final divergence of approaches.

9. COMPARATIVE VERSUS NONCOMPARATIVE EVALUATION

The result of attempts to evaluate recent new curricula has been remarkably uniform; comparing students taking the old curriculum with students taking the new one, it usually appears that students using the new curriculum do rather better on the examinations designed for that curriculum and rather worse on those designed for the old curriculum, while students using the old curriculum perform in the opposite way. Certainly, there is a remarkable absence of striking improvements on the same criteria (with some exceptions, of which the most notable is the performance of students in studies of good programmed texts). Initially, one's tendency is to feel that the mountain has labored and brought forth a mouse — and that it is a positive mouse and not a negative one entirely depends upon the evaluation of the criteria, i.e., (mainly) tests used. A legitimate reaction is to look very seriously into the question of whether one should not weight the judged merit of content and goals by subject-matter experts a great deal more heavily than small differences in level of performance on unassessed criteria. If we do this, then relatively minor improvements in performance, on the right goals, become very valuable, and in these terms the new curriculum looks considerably better. Whether this alteration of weights can really be justified is a matter that needs very serious investigation; it requires a rather careful analysis of the real importance to the understanding and use of contemporary physics, as it is seen by, e.g., physicists, of the missing elements in the old curriculum. It is all too tempting to feel that the reweighting must be correct because one is so thoroughly convinced that the new course is better.

Another legitimate reaction is to wonder whether the examinations are really doing a good job testing the depth of understanding of the people trained on the new curriculum. Here the use of the oversize question pool becomes extremely important. Cronbach speaks of a 700-item pool (without flinching!) and this is surely the order of magnitude that makes sense in terms of a serious evaluation of a one- or two-year curriculum. Again, it is going to be tempting to put items into the pool that reflect mere differences of terminology in the new course, for example. Of course if the pool consists mainly of questions of that kind, the new-curriculum students will do much better. But their superiority will be almost entirely illusory. Cronbach warns us against this risk of course-dependent terminology, although he goes too far in segregating understanding from terminology (this point is taken up below). So here, too, we must be certain to use external evaluators in the construction or assessment of the question pool.

Illegitimate reactions run from the charming suggestion that such results simply demonstrate the weaknesses of evaluation techniques, to a more interesting suggestion implicit in Cronbach's paper. He says:

> Since group comparisons give equivocal results, I believe that a formal study should be designed primarily to determine the post-course performance of a well-described group, with respect to many important objectives and side-effects.[5]

Cronbach is apparently about to suggest a way in which we can avoid comparison, not with goals or objectives, but with another group, supposedly matched on relevant variables. What is this noncomparative alternative procedure for evaluation? He continues:

> Ours is a problem like that of the engineer examining a new automobile. He can set himself the task of defining its performance characteristics and its dependability. It would be merely distracting to put his question in the form: 'Is this car better or worse than the competing brand?'

---

[5]This and the succeeding quotation are from p. 238.

It is perfectly true that the automobile engineer *might* only just be interested in the question of the performance and dependability of the new automobile. But no automobile engineer ever has had this pure interest, and no automobile engineer ever will have it. Objectives do not become "important" except in a context of practical choice. Unrealistic objectives, for example, are not important. The very measures of the performance and dependability of an automobile and our interest in them spring *entirely* from knowledge of what has and has not so far proved possible, or possible within a certain price-class, or possible with certain interior space, or with a certain overall weight, etc. The use of calibrated instruments is not an alternative to, but only a mediated way of, doing comparative studies. The same applies in the field of curriculum development. We already have curricula aimed at almost every subject known to man, and there isn't any real interest in producing curricula for curricula's sake; to the extent that there is, there isn't any interest in evaluating them. We are interested in curricula because they may prove to be better than what we now have, in some important way. We may assign someone the task of rating a curriculum on certain variables, without asking them simultaneously to look up the performance of other curricula on these variables. But when we come to *evaluate* the curriculum, as opposed to merely describing its performance, then we inevitably confront the question of its superiority or inferiority to the competition. To say it's a "valuable contribution," a "desirable" or "useful" course, even to say—in the usual context—that it's very good, is to imply relative merit. Indeed the very scales we use to measure its performance are often percentile scales or others with a built-in comparison.

There are even important reasons for putting the question in its comparative form immediately. Comparative evaluations are often very much easier than noncomparative evaluations, because we can often use tests which yield differences instead of having to find an absolute scale and then eventually compare the absolute scores. If we are discussing chess-teaching courses, for example, we might match two groups for background variables, and then let them play each other off in a round-robin tournament. Attempting to devise a measure of skill of an absolute kind would be a nightmare, but we might easily get consistent and significant differences from this kind of comparative evaluation. Cronbach is not making the "pure pay-off" mistake of thinking that one can avoid all reference to general goals; but he is proposing an approach which underestimates the implicit comparative element in any field of social engineering including automobile assessment and curriculum evaluation, just as the pay-off approach underestimates the implicit appeal to abstract intermediate qualities.

Cronbach continues in this paragraph with a line of thought about which there can be no disagreement at all; he points out that in any cases of comparisons between importantly different teaching instruments, no real understanding of the reason for a difference in performance is gained from the discovery that one of them *is* notably superior to the other: "No one knows which of the ingredients is responsible for the advantages." But understanding is not our *only* goal in evaluation. We are also interested in questions of support, encouragement, adoption, reward, refinement, etc. And these extremely important questions can be given a useful though in some cases not a complete answer by the mere discovery of superiority. It will be recalled that in an earlier section we argued that the pure pay-off position suffers by comparison with the supporter of mediated evaluation in that his results will not include the data we need in order to locate sources of difficulty, etc. Here Cronbach is arguing that his noncomparative approach will be more likely to give us the data we need for future improvement. But this is not in any way an advantage of the noncomparative method as such. It is simply an advantage of methods in which more variables are examined in more detail. If we want to pin down the exact reasons for differences between programs, it is quite true that "small-scale, well-controlled studies can profitably be used to compare alternative versions of the same course" whereas the large-scale overall comparison will not be so valuable. But that in no way eliminates the need for comparative studies at some point in our evaluation procedures. In short, his argument is simply that in order to get *explanations,* one needs more control groups, and possibly more short-run studies, than one needs for summative *evaluation.* This is incontestible; but it does not show that for the purposes of overall evaluation we can or should avoid overall comparison.

One might put the point in terms of the following analogy: in the history of automobile engine design there have been a number of occasions when a designer has turned out an engine that was quite inexplicably superior to the competition—the Kettering GM V8, the Coventry Climax and the Weslake Ford conversions are well-known examples. Perhaps thirty variables are significantly changed in the design of any new engine and for a long time after these had been in production nobody, including the designer, knew which of them had been mainly responsible for the improvement. But the decision to go into production, the decision to put the further research into the engine that led to finding out what made it great, indeed the beginning of a new era in engine design, required *only the comparative evaluation*. You set a great team to work and you hope they are going to strike gold; but then you assay the ore before you start the big capital expenditure involved in finding out the configuration of the lode and mining. This is the way we have to work in any field where there are too many variables and too little time.

10. PRACTICAL PROCEDURES FOR CONTROL-GROUP EVALUATION

It is a major theme of Cronbach's that control group comparisons in the curriculum game are not really very suitable. We have just seen how his attempt to provide a positive alternative does not develop into a realistic answer in the context of typical evaluation enquiries. It is therefore appropriate for us to attempt to meet some of the objections that he raises to the control group method since we are recommending that this be left in possession of the field.

The suggestion that gross comparisons yield only small differences must first be met, as indicated above (and as Cronbach recommends elsewhere), by increasing the power of the microscope—that is, by increasing the type and number of items that are being tested, increasing the size of the group in order to get more reliability into differences that do appear, and developing new and more appropriate tests where the present ones seem to be the weakness. And where we pin down a beneficial factor, we then attempt to rewrite with more emphasis on it, to magnify the gain. But once all this has been said, the fact remains that it is probably the case that we shall often have to proceed in terms of rather small differences; that producing large differences will usually require a multiple-push approach, one that attacks not only the curriculum but the student-grouping procedures, the teacher presentation, the classroom time allocation, seeking above all to develop positive feedback via the long-term effects that improvements in every subject in the school curriculum will eventually produce for us—a general increase in the level of interest and preparedness. This is not too depressing a prospect, and it is exactly paralleled in that other field in which we attempt to change human behavior by applying pressure on the subjects for a few hours a week over a period of one or several years—the field of psychotherapy. We are perhaps too used to the discovery of miracle drugs or technological breakthroughs in the aerospace field to recognize the atypicality of such (apparently) "instant progress." Even in the automobile engineering field, to stay with Cronbach's example, it is a well-known theorem that developing a good established design yields better results than introducing a promising but radically new design in about twice as many cases as engineers under forty are willing to believe. What one may reasonably expect as the reward for work is *not* great leaps and bounds, but slow and steady improvement. And of course we shall sometimes go down dead ends. Cronbach says that "formally designed experiments pitting one course against another are rarely definitive enough to justify their cost" but he does not allow sufficiently for the fact that the lack of definite results is often just the kind of knowledge that we need. If we have really satisfied ourselves that we are using good tests of the main criterion variable (and we surely can manage that, with care) then to discover parity of performance *is* to have discovered something extremely informative. "No difference" is not "no knowledge."

Of course, we cannot conclude from a null result that all the techniques involved in a new curriculum are worthless improvements. We must go on to make the micro-studies that will enable us to see whether any one of them is worthwhile. But we have discovered something very significant. Doing the gross comparative study is going to cost the same whatever kind of results we get, and we have to do it sooner or later. Of course it is absurd to stop after discovering an insignificant difference; we must continue in the direction of further analytical research, of the kind Cronbach enthusiastically recommends. The impact of his article is to suggest the unimportance of the control group study, whereas the case can only be made for its inadequacy as a *total* approach to *the whole of* curriculum research.[6] We shall here try to provide some practical suggestions for experimental designs that will yield more than a gross comparative evaluation.

A significant part of the reason for Cronbach's despair over comparative studies lies in his recognition that we are unable to arrange for double-blind conditions. "In an educational experi-

---

[6]Yet he does agree with the necessity for making the practical decisions, e.g. between textbooks (p. 232), for which nothing less than a valid comparative study is adequate.

ment it is difficult to keep people unaware that they are an experimental group. And it is quite impossible to neutralize the biases of the teacher as those of the doctor are neutralized in the double-blind design. It is thus never certain whether any observed advantage is attributable to the educational innovation as such, or to the greater energy that teachers and students put forth when a method is fresh and 'experimental.'" (p. 237). But Cronbach despairs too quickly. The analogy in the medical field is not with drug studies, where we are fortunate enough to be able to achieve double-blind conditions, but with psychotherapy studies where the therapist is obviously endowed with enthusiasm for his treatment, and the patient cannot be kept in ignorance of whether he is getting some kind of treatment. If Cronbach's reasoning is correct, it would not be possible to design an adequate psychotherapy outcome study. But it *is* possible to design such a study, and the way to do it – as far as this point goes[7] – is to use more than one comparison group. If we use only one control group, we cannot tell whether it's the enthusiasm or the experimental technique that explains a difference. But if we use several experimental groups, we can estimate the size of the enthusiasm effect. We make comparisons between a number of therapy groups, in each of which the therapist is enthusiastic, but in each of which the method of therapy is radically different. As far as possible, one should employ forms of therapy in which directly incompatible procedures are adopted, and as far as possible match the patients allocated to each type (close matching is not important). There are a number of therapies on the market which meet the first condition in several dimensions, and it is easy enough to develop pseudo-therapies which would be promising enough to be enthusiasm-generating for some practitioners (e.g. newly graduated internists inducted into the experimental program for a short period). The method of differences plus the method of concomitant variations (analysis of covariance) will then assist us in drawing conclusions about whether enthusiasm is the (or a) major factor in therapeutic success, even though double-blind conditions are unobtainable. Nor is this the only kind of design which can do this; other approaches are available (one more is discussed below), and ingenious experimenters will doubtless think of still more, to enable us to handle this kind of research problem. There is nothing indispensable about the double-blind study.

---

[7]Other difficulties are discussed in more detail in "The Experimental Investigation of Psychoanalysis" in *Psychoanalysis, Scientific Method and Philosophy*, S. Hook (Ed.), New York: NYU Press, 1959.

oh?

It is true that the curriculum field is slightly more difficult than the psychotherapy field, because it is harder to meet the condition of excluding common elements from the several comparison groups. Although the average intelligent patient will accept almost any nonsense as a form of therapy, thanks to the witchdoctor tradition, need to be healed, etc., it is not equally easy to convince students and teachers that they are receiving and giving instruction in geometry unless what is going on really is a kind of geometry that makes some sense. And if it is, then interpretation of one of the possible outcomes is ambiguous, i.e., if several groups do about as well, it may be *either* because enthusiasm does the trick, or because the common content is efficacious. However, comparative evaluation is still well worthwhile, because if we find a very marked *difference* between the groups, when enthusiasm on the part of the teachers and students occurs in both cases, we may be reasonably sure that the difference is due to the curriculum content. And it is surely possible to vary presentation sequence, methods, difficulty, example, etc., enough so that indistinguishable results are improbable.

Now it is not particularly difficult to arrange for the enthusiasm matching. Corresponding to the cut-rate "new therapy" comparison groups, where the therapy procedures are brainstormed up in a day or two of wild free-associating by the experimenters assisted by a lot of beer and some guilt-ridden eclectic therapists, we set up some cut-rate "new curricula" in the following way. First, we get two bright graduate students or instructors in (let us suppose) economics, give them a vocabulary list for the tenth grade and pay them $500 a chapter for a translation of Samuelson's text into tenth grade language, encouraging them to use their originality in introducing the new ideas. They could probably handle the whole text in a summer and so for a few thousand dollars, including costs of reproducing pilot materials, we have something we could set up against one of the fancier economics curricula, based on a great deal of high-priced help and laborious field-testing. Then we find a couple of really bright college juniors, majoring in economics, from different colleges, and give *them* a summer to turn their recent experience at the receiving end of introductory economics courses, and their current direct acquaintance with the problems of concept grasping in the field, into a curriculum outline (filled in as much as possible) of a brief introduction to economics for the tenth-grade, not centered around any particular text. And for a third comparison group we locate some enthusiasts for one of the *current* secondary school texts in "economics" and have them work on a revision of it with the author(s) and in the light of some sampling of their colleagues' reactions to the text in class use.

Preferably using the curriculum-makers as teachers (*pace* State Departments of Education) we then turn them loose on loosely matched comparison groups, in school systems geographically well removed from the ones where we are running the tests on the high-priced spread. We might toss in a little incentive payment in the way of a preannounced bonus for these groups if they don't get significantly outscored by the supercurriculum. Now then, if we *still* get a big difference in favor of the supercurriculum, we have good reason for thinking that we have taken care of the enthusiasm variable. Moreover we don't have to pull this stunt with every kind of subject matter, since enthusiasm is presumably reasonably (though definitely not entirely) constant in its effects across subject matter. At any rate, a modest sampling should suffice to check this.

One of the nice things about this kind of comparative study is that even if we get the slightly ambiguous negligible-difference result, which will leave us in doubt as to whether a common enthusiasm is responsible for the result, or whether a roughly comparable job in teaching economics is being done by all the curricula, we get a nice economic bonus. If we can whomp up new curricula on a shoestring which are going to produce pretty good results, so much the better; we can do it often and thereby keep up the supply of enthusiasm-stoked project directors, and increase the chances of hitting on some really new big-jackpot approach from a Newton of curriculum reform.

Moreover, still on a shoestring, we can settle the question of enthusiasm fairly quickly even in the event of a tie between the various curricula, by dumping them into the lap of some *antagonistic* and some *neutral* teachers to use during the next school year or two, while on the other hand arranging for the original curriculum-makers to lovingly train a small group of highly selected and innovation-inclined teachers to do the same job. Comparisons between the performance of these three new groups and that of the old ones should enable us to pin down the role of enthusiasm rather precisely, and in addition the no-doubt variable immunity of the various curricula to lack of enthusiasm.

A few obvious elaborations of the above procedures, including an opportunity for the novice curriculum-makers to spend a couple of afternoons on field-testing early sections of their new curriculum to give them some "feel" for the speed at which students at this level can grasp new concepts, the use of some care in selecting teachers for their conservatism, allergy, or lethargy, using self-ratings plus peer-ratings plus attitude inventories, would of course be incorporated in an actual study.

The enthusiasm "difficulty" here is simply an example of what we might call *measurement-interference effects* (or coupled-variable phenomena), of which the placebo effect in medicine and the Hawthorne effect in industrial and social psychology are well-known instances. In each case we are interested in finding out the effects of a certain factor, but we cannot introduce the factor into the experimental situation without producing a disturbance which may itself be responsible for the observed changes. In the drug field, the disturbance consists in the act of giving the patient something which he considers to be a drug, an event which does not ordinarily happen to him, and which consequently may produce effects of its own, quite apart from the "intrinsic" effects of the drug. In the Hawthorne effect, the disturbance is the alteration of, e.g., conditions of work, which may suggest to the worker that he is the subject of special study and interest, and *this* may lead to improved output, rather than the physical changes in the environment which are the intended control variables under study.

The cases so far mentioned are all ones where the beliefs of the subjects are the mediating factor between the disturbance and the ambiguous effects. This is characteristic in the field of psychology, but the situation is not essentially different from that occurring in technological research where we face problems such as the absorption of heat by a thermometer which thereby alters the temperature that it is supposedly measuring. That is, some of the effect observed (which is here the eventual length of the mercury column) is due to the fact that in order to get a measurement at all you have to alter what you are trying to measure. The measuring process introduces another physical object into proximity with the measured object, and the instrument itself has a certain heat capacity, a factor in whose influence you are not interested, though in order to find out what you do need to know you eventually have to make an estimate of the magnitude of the measurement-interference effect. The ingenious double-blind design is only appropriate in certain circumstances, and is only one of many ways in which we can compensate for these effects. It therefore seems unduly pessimistic of Cronbach to suppose that the impossibility of a double blind in curriculum work is fatal to comparative evaluation. Indeed, when he comes to discuss follow-up studies, he agrees that comparative work is essential (p. 240). The conclusion seems obligatory that comparative evaluation, mediated or not, is the method of choice for evaluation problems.

11. CRITERIA OF EDUCATIONAL ACHIEVEMENT FOR EVALUATION STUDIES

We may now turn to the problem of specifying in more detail the criteria which should be used in evaluating a teaching instrument. The check-list to follow serves as a useful mnemonic for the goal-formulator and consistency-analyst. We may retain Bloom's (Bloom et al., 1956) convenient trichotomy of cognitive, affective, and motor variables, though we shall often refer to the last two as motivational and physical or nonmental variables, but under the first two of these we shall propose a rather different structure, especially under the knowledge and understanding subdivisions of the cognitive field.

Some preliminary notes follow:

(i) It should be stressed at the beginning that the word "knowledge" *can* be used to cover understanding (or comprehension) and even affective conditions ("knowing how it feels to be completely rejected by one's peer group"), but that it is here used in the sense in which it can be *contrasted* with comprehension and experience or valuation, i.e., in the sense in which we think of it as "mere knowledge." Comprehension or understanding, in terms of this contrast, refers to a psychological state involving knowledge, not of one item, nor of several separate items, but of a field. A field or structure is a set of items related in a systematic way, and knowledge of the field involves knowledge not only of the items but of their relations. Understanding particular items in a field requires knowledge of the relation of the item to other items in the field, i.e., some knowledge of the field. A field is often open-ended in the sense of having potential reference or applicability to an indefinite number of future examples. In this latter case, comprehension involves the capacity to apply to these novel cases the appropriate rule, rubric or concept. A field may be a field of abstract or practical knowledge, of thought or of skills: one may understand the field of patent law, or how to retime two-stroke engines.

(ii) With respect to any field of knowledge we can distinguish between a relatively abstract or *conceptual* description of the parameters (which are to occupy the role of dependent variables in our study) and a *manifestation* description, the latter being the next stage towards the specification of the particular tests to be used, which we may call the *operational* description. It is appropriate to describe the criteria at all three levels, although we finally apply only the third, just as it is appropriate to give the steps of a difficult proof in mathematics, because it shows us the conceptual foundations for adopting the particular final step proposed.

(iii) I have followed the usual practice here in listing positive goals (with the possible exception of the example in 5) but a word of caution is in order. Although most negatively desired effects are the absence of positively desired effects, this is not always true, and more generally we often wish to alter the weighting of a variable when it drops below a certain level. For example, we may not be worried if we get *no* change on socialization with a course that is working well in the cognitive domain, and we may give small credit for *large gains* in this dimension. But if it produces a marked rise in sociopathic behavior (i.e., large losses) we may regard this as a fatal defect in the course. The same applies to a by-product like forgetting or rejection of material in other subject areas. Another example is discussed below.

(iv) A word about originality or "creativity"; this may be manifested in a problem-solving skill, as an artistic skill (which combines motor and perceptual and perhaps verbal skills) and in many other ways. On the whole it seems as mistaken to make it a separate criterion as to make "cleverness" one.

(v) In general, I have tried to reduce the acknowledged overlap among the factors identified in Bloom's analysis, and am prepared to pay a price for this desideratum, if such a price must be paid. There are many reasons for avoiding overlap, of which one of the more important and perhaps less obvious ones is that when the comparative weighting of criteria is undertaken for a given subject, independence greatly simplifies the process, since a straight weighting by individual merit will overweight the hidden loading factors.

(vi) There is still a tendency in the literature to regard factual recall and knowledge of terminology with general disdain. But for many subjects, a very substantial score on that dimension is an absolutely necessary condition for adequate performance. This is not the same as saying that a sufficiently high score on that scale will compensate for lack of understanding, even where we use a single index compounded from the weighted scores: we must taper off the weighting in the upper ranges of the recall scales. There are other subjects, especially mathematics and physics, where knowing how to apply the terminology requires and hence guarantees a very deep understanding and terminology-free tests are just bad tests. (cf. Cronbach, p. 245)

11.1 CONCEPTUAL DESCRIPTION OF EDUCATIONAL OBJECTIVES

1. Knowledge, of

    a. Items of specific information including definitions of terms in the field.

    b. Sequences or patterns of items of information including sets of rules, procedures or classifications for handling or evaluating items of information (we are here talking about mere knowledge of the rule or classification and not the capacity to apply it).

2. Comprehension or Understanding, of

    a. Internal relationships in the field,[8] i.e., the way in which some of the knowledge claims are consequences of others and imply yet others, the way in which the terminology applies within the field; in short what might be called understanding of the intrafield syntax of the field or subfield.

    b. Interfield relations, i.e., relations between the knowledge claims in this field and those in other fields; what we might call the interfield syntax.

    c. Application of the field or the rules, procedures, and concepts of the field to appropriate examples, where the field is one that has such applications; this might be called the semantics of the field.

3. Motivation (Attitude/values/affect)

    a. Attitudes toward the course, e.g. acoustics.

    b. Attitudes toward the subject, e.g. physics.

    c. Attitudes toward the field, e.g. science.

    d. Attitudes toward material to which the field is relevant, e.g. increased skepticism about usual advertising claims about "high fidelity" from miniature radios (connection with 2c above).

    e. Attitudes toward learning, reading, discussing, enquiring in general, etc.

---

[8]Typically, "the field" should be construed more widely than "the subject" since we are very interested in transfer from one subject to related ones and rate a course better to the extent it facilitates this. In rating transfer, we can range very far, e.g., from a course on psychology to reactions to commercials showing white-coated men.

f. Attitudes toward the school.
g. Attitudes toward teaching as a career, teacher status, etc.
h. Attitudes toward (feelings about, etc.) the teacher as a person.
i. Attitude toward classmates, attitude toward society (obvious further subheadings).
j. Attitude toward self, e.g., increase of realistic self-appraisal (which also involves cognitive domain).

4. Nonmental Abilities

a. Perceptual.
b. Psycho-motor.
c. Motor, including, e.g., some sculpting skills.
d. Social skills.

5. Noneducational Variables

There are a number of noneducational goals, usually implicit, which are served by many existing courses and even by new courses, and some of them are even justifiable in special circumstances as, e.g., in a prison. The crudest example is the "keeps 'em out of mischief" view of schooling. Others include the use of the schools to handle unemployment problems, to provide a market for textbook sales. It is realistic to remember that these criteria may be quite important to parents, teachers, publishers, and authors even if not to children.

11.2 MANIFESTATION DIMENSIONS OF CRITERIAL VARIABLES

1. Knowledge

In the sense described above, this is evinced by
a. Recital skills.
b. Discrimination skills.
c. Completion skills.
d. Labeling skills.
Note: Where immediate performance changes are not discernible, there may still be some subliminal capacity, manifesting itself in a reduction in relearning time, i.e., time for future learning to criterion.

2. Comprehension

This is manifested on some of the above types of performance and also on

a. Analyzing skills, including laboratory analysis skills, other than motor, as well as the verbal analytic skills exhibited in criticism, précis, etc.
b. Synthesizing skills.
c. Evaluation skills, including self-appraisal.
d. Problem-solving skills (speed-dependent and speed-independent).

3. Attitude

Manifestations usually involve simultaneous demonstration of some cognitive acquisition. The kinds of instrument involved are questionnaires, projective tests, Q-sorts, experimental choice situations, and normal lifetime choice situations (choice of college major, career, spouse, friends, etc.). Each of the attitudes mentioned is characteristically identifiable on a passive to active dimension (related to the distinctions expounded on in Bloom, but disregarding extent of systematization of value system which can be treated as a (meta-) cognitive skill).

4. The Nonmental Abilities

All are exhibited in performances of various kinds, which again can be either artificially elicited or extracted from life-history. Typical examples are the capacity to speak in an organized way in front of an audience, to criticize a point of view (not previously heard) in an effective way, etc. (This again connects with the ability conceptually described under 2c).

11.3 FOLLOW-UP

The time dimension is a crucial element in the analysis of performance and one that deserves an extensive independent investigation. Retention, recall, depth of understanding, extent of imprinting, can all be tested by reapplications of the tests or observations used to determine the instantaneous peak performance, on the dimensions indicated above. However, some follow-up criteria are not repetitions of earlier tests or observations;

eventual choice of career, longevity of marriage, extent of adult social service, career success, are relevant and important variables which require case history investigation. But changes of habits and character are often not separate variables, being simply long-term changes on cognitive and affective scales.

11.4 SECONDARY EFFECTS

A serious deficiency of previous studies of new curricula has been a failure to sample the teacher population adequately. When perfecting a teaching instrument, we cannot justify generalizing from pilot studies unless not only the students but the teachers are fair samples of the intended population. This need to pre-dict/select favorable classroom performance for the new materials also underlines the importance of studies of measurement-interference effects. Just as generalizing has been based upon inadequate analysis of the teacher sample, so criterion discussions have not paid sufficient attention to teacher benefits. It is quite wrong to evaluate a teaching instrument without any consideration of the effects on the operator as well as on the subjects. In an obvious sense, the operator *is* one of the subjects.

We may distinguish secondary effects (i.e., those on others than the students taking the course) from tertiary effects. Secondary effects are those arising from or because of direct exposure to the material, and it is mainly the teachers and teachers' helpers who are affected in this way. Tertiary effects are those effects on the school or other students brought about by someone who exhibits the primary or secondary effects.

11.41 EFFECTS ON THE TEACHER

A new curriculum may have very desirable effects on updating a teacher's knowledge or pedagogy, with subsequent pay-off in various ways including the better education of other classes at a later stage (a tertiary effect), whether he/she is there using the old curriculum or the new one. Similarly, it may have very bad effects on the teacher, perhaps through induction of fatigue, or through failing to leave her any feeling of status or significant role in the classroom (as did some programmed texts), etc.

It is easy to itemize a number of such considerations, and we really need a minor study of the taxonomy of these secondary effects under each of their several headings. Interestingly, what I have called the interference effects, e.g., those due to enthusiasm, may be of immediate value themselves. Very often the introduction of new curriculum material is tied to teacher in-service training institutes or special in-service training interviews. These of course have effects on the teacher herself with respect to status, self-concept, pay, interests, etc., and indirectly on later students. Many of these effects on the teacher show up in her other activities; at the college level there will normally be some serious reduction of research time resulting from association with an experimental curriculum, and this may have results for promotion expectations in either the positive or the negative direction, depending upon departmental policy. All of these results are effects of the new curriculum, at least for a long time, and in certain circumstances they may be sufficiently important to count rather heavily against other advantages. Involvement with curricula of a highly controversial kind may have such strongly damaging secondary effects for the teacher as to raise questions as to whether it is proper to refer to it as a good curriculum for schools in the social context in which these secondary effects are so bad.

11.42 EFFECTS ON TEACHER'S COLLEAGUES

Tertiary effects are the effects on people other than those directly exposed to the curriculum: once again they may be highly significant. A simple example of a tertiary effect involves other members of the staff who may be called upon to teach less attractive courses, or more courses, or whose load may be reduced for reasons of parity, or who may be stimulated by discussions with the experimental group teachers, etc. In many cases, effects of this kind will vary widely from situation to situation, and such effects may then be less appropriately thought of as effects of the curriculum (although even the primary effects of this, i.e., the effects on the students, will vary widely geographically and temporally) but there will sometimes be constancies in these effects which will require recognition as characteristic effects of this particular teaching instrument. This will of course be noticeable in the case of controversial experimental courses, but it will also be significant where the course bears on problems of school administration, relation of the subject to other subjects, and so on. Good evaluation requires some attempt to identify effects of this kind.

11.43 EFFECTS ON OTHER STUDENTS

Another tertiary effect, already referred to in discussing the effect of the curriculum on the teacher, is the effect on other students. Just as a teacher may be improved by exposure to a new curriculum, and this improvement may show up in benefits for students that she has in other classes, or at a later period using the old curriculum, etc., so there may be an effect of the curriculum on students not in the experimental class through the intermediary of *students* who are. Probably more pronounced in a boarding school or small college, the communication between students is still a powerful enough instrument in ordinary circumstances for this to be a significant influence. The students may of course be influenced in other ways; there may be additions to the library as a result of the funds available for the new course that represent values for the other students, etc. All of these are educationally significant effects of the course adoption.

11.44 EFFECTS ON ADMINISTRATORS

The school administrators may be affected by new teaching instruments in various ways: their powers of appointment may be curtailed, if the teaching instrument's efficiency will reduce faculty; they may acquire increased prestige (or nuisance) through the use of the school as an experimental laboratory; they may find this leads to more (or less) trouble with the parents or alumni or legislators; the pay-off through more national scholarships may be a value to them, either intrinsically or incidentally to some other end, etc. Again, it is obvious that in certain special cases this variable will be a very important part of the total set that are affected by the new instrument, and evaluation must include some recognition of this possibility. It is not so much the factors common to the use of novel material, but the course-specific effects that particularly require estimation and almost every new science or social studies course has such effects.

11.45 EFFECTS ON PARENTS

Effects on the parents are of course well known, but they tend to be regarded as mainly nuisance-generating effects. On the contrary, many such effects should be regarded as part of the adult education program in which this country is still highly deficient. In some subjects, e.g. Russian, there is unlikely to be a very significant effect, but in the field of problems of democracy, elementary accounting, and literature this may be a most important effect.

11.46 EFFECTS ON THE SCHOOL OR COLLEGE

Many of these are covered above, particularly under the heading of effects on the administrator, but there are of course some effects that are more readily classified under this heading, such as improvement in facilities, support, spirit, applicants, integration, etc.

11.47 EFFECTS ON THE TAXPAYER

These are partly considered in the section on costs below, but certain points are worth mentioning. We are using the term taxpayer and not ratepayer here to indicate a reference to the total tax structure, and the most important kinds of effects here are the possibility of very large-scale emulation of a given curriculum reform project, which in toto, especially with evaluation on the scale envisioned here, is likely to add a substantial amount to the overall tax burden. For the unmarried or childless taxpayer, this will be an effect which may with some grounds be considered a social injustice. Insofar as evaluation of a national armament program must be directly tied to questions of fair and unfair tax loads, the same must be applied in any national considerations of very large-scale curriculum reforms.

12. VALUES AND COSTS

12.1 RANGE OF UTILITY

No evaluation of a teaching instrument can be considered complete without reference to the range of its applicability and the importance of improvement of education in that range. If we are particularly concerned with the underprivileged groups, then it will be a value of considerable importance if our new teaching instrument is especially well adapted for that group. Its utility may not be very highly generalizable, but that may be offset by the special social utility of the effects actually obtained. Similarly, the fact that the instrument is demonstrably usable by teachers with no extra training sharply increases its short-term utility. Indeed it may be so important as to make it one of the goals of instrument development, for short-run high-yield improvements.

12.2 MORAL CONSIDERATIONS

Considerations of the kind that are normally referred to as moral have a place in the evaluation of new curricula. If the procedures for grading, or treating students in class (the use of scapegoats, for example), although pedagogically effective, are unjust, then we may have grounds for judging the instrument undesirable which are independent of any directly testable consequences. If one conceives of morality as a system of principles aimed at maximizing long-run social utility, based on an egalitarian axiom, then moral evaluations will usually show up somewhere else on the criteria given above, as primary or secondary effects. But the time lag before they do so may be so long as to make it appropriate for us to introduce this as a separate category. There are a number of other features of teaching instruments to which we react morally; "the dehumanizing influence of teaching machines" is a description often used by critics who are partly affected by moral considerations; whether misguidedly or not is a question that must be faced. Curricula stressing the difference in performance on the standardized intelligence tests of Negro and white children have been attacked as morally undesirable, and the same has been said of textbooks in which the role of the United States in world history has been viewed somewhat critically. Considerations like this will of course show up on a content-mediated approach to evaluation but they deserve a separate entry because the reaction is not to the truth or insight provided by the program, but to some other consequences of providing what may well be truths or insights, namely the consequences involving the welfare of the society as a whole.

12.3 COSTS

The costing of curriculum adoption is a rather poorly researched affair. Enthusiasts for new curricula tend to overlook a large number of secondary costs that arise, not only in the experimental situation, but in the event of large-scale adoption. Evaluation, particularly of items for purchase from public funds, should have a strong commitment to examination of the cost situation. Most of the appropriate analysis can be best obtained from an experienced industrial accountant, but it is perhaps worth mentioning here that even when the money has been provided for the salaries of curriculum-makers and field-testers and in-service training institutes there are a number of other costs that are not easily assessed, such as the costs of rearrangements of curriculum, differential loads on other faculty, diminished availability for supervisory chores of the experimental staff (and in the long run, where the instrument requires more of the teacher's time than the one it replaces, this becomes a permanent cost), the "costs" of extra demands on *student time* (presumably at the expense of other courses they might be taking), and of energy drain on the faculty as they acquire the necessary background and skills in the new curriculum, and so on through the list of other indirect effects, many of which have cost considerations attached, whether the cost is in dollars or some other valuable.

13. A MARGINAL KIND OF "EVALUATION" – "EXPLANATORY EVALUATION"

Data relevant to the variables outlined in the preceding section are the basic elements for almost all types of evaluation. But sometimes, as was indicated in the fourth section, evaluation refers to *interpretation* or *explanation*. While not considering this to be a primary or even a fully proper sense, it is clear from the literature that there is some tendency to extend the term in this direction. It seems preferable to distinguish between evaluation and the attempt to discover an explanation of certain kinds of result, even when both are using the same data. Explanation-hunting is sometimes part of process research and sometimes part of other areas in the field of educational research. When we turn to considerations of this kind, data of a quite different variety are called for. We shall, for example, need to have information about specific skills and attitudes of the students who perform in a particular way; we shall call upon the assistance of experts who—or tests which—may be able to demonstrate that the failure of a particular teaching instrument is due to its use of an inappropriately advanced vocabulary, rather than to any lack of comprehensible organization. Evaluation of this kind, however, is and should be secondary to evaluation of the kinds discussed previously, for the same reason and in the same sense that therapy is secondary to diagnosis.

14. CONCLUSIONS

The aim of this paper has been to move one step further in the direction of an adequate methodology of curriculum evaluation. It is clear that taking this step involves considerable complication of the model of an adequate evaluation study by comparison with what has passed under this heading all too frequently in the past. Further analysis of the problem may reveal even greater difficulties that must be sorted out with an attendant increase in complexity. Complex experiments on the scale we have been discussing are very expensive in both time and effort. But it has been an important part of the argument of this paper that no substitutes will do. If we want to know the answers to the questions that matter about new teaching instruments, we have got to do experiments which will yield those answers. The educational profession is suffering from a completely inappropriate conception of the cost scale for educational research. To develop a new automobile engine or a rocket engine is a very, very expensive business despite the extreme constancy in the properties of physical substances. When we are dealing with a teaching instrument such as a new curriculum or classroom procedure, with its extreme dependence upon highly variable operators and recipients, we must expect considerably more expense. The social pay-off is enormously more important, and this society can, in the long run, afford the expense. At the moment the main deficiency is trained evaluation manpower, so that short-term transition to the appropriate scale of investigation is possible only in rare cases. But the long-term transition must be made. We are dealing with something more important and more difficult to evaluate than an engine design, and we are attempting to get by with something like 1 per cent of the cost of developing an engine design. The educational profession as a whole has a primary obligation to recognize the difficulty of good curriculum development with its essential concomitant, evaluation, and to begin a unified attack on the problem of financing the kind of improvement that may help us towards the goal of a few million enlightened citizens on the earth's surface, even at the expense of one on the surface of Mars.

Aspects of Curriculum Evaluation: A Synopsis

J. Stanley Ahmann
Colorado State University

A review of the major points contained in the contributions to this monograph concerning curriculum evaluation reemphasizes the all too obvious fact that, from any angle that it is to be viewed, the problem of curriculum evaluation is enormous. Indeed, perhaps in the minds of some it is better described as horrendous. There is general agreement as to some of its major problems. For example, most will agree that far too little attention is paid to curriculum evaluation and, as a result, far too little time is allowed for this function and far too little progress is now being realized. Moreover, much of the work that is being accomplished can be classified as less than top quality. Finally, a variety of strategies could be applied, yet some are largely unused.

Concern is expressed with regard to curriculum evaluation processes. There is a major need for development of evaluation strategies which are suitable for specific evaluation purposes. Perhaps lack of experience in formal evaluation of curricula causes some educators to lean too heavily on instruments developed to identify the degree of individual differences existing among students.

The main theme of the paper prepared by Tyler is, in a sense, a summary of many of the concerns which now exist. Tyler believes that "the accelerating development of research in the area of educational evaluation has created a collection of concepts, facts, generalizations, and research instruments and methods that represent many inconsistencies and contradictions because new problems, new conditions, and new assumptions are introduced without reviewing the changes they create in the relevance and logic of the older structure." Certainly the notion that evaluation is a crucial activity in education is not new. On the other hand, the notion that it be applied regularly in the development of curricula is not as widely accepted today as it ought to be. Very likely, this creates many of the new problems, new conditions, and new assumptions to which Tyler refers.

Considerable sophistication exists with regard to evaluation efforts aimed at the individual student. Whether these methods are appropriate to program evaluation is another matter. Experience continues to show that the methods commonly applied in student-oriented evaluation are not always adapted with ease to program-oriented evaluation. Herein lie many of the roots of our problem.

The contributors to this monograph have attempted to sort out a number of important concepts needed as "building stones" in the development of program evaluation. These have considerable potential with respect to the task of reducing some of the confusion which exists. As a first step, we certainly need a clear concept of that which is to be evaluated; more specifically, the curriculum. Secondly, we need clarification, at least in a general way, of the methodological approaches available to us as we face various evaluation problems.

DEFINITION OF CURRICULUM

Perhaps it seems unnecessary to raise the question as to the definition of the term "curriculum." This term, however, can be deceptively difficult for some. The definition provided by Gagné is useful. He believes that "a curriculum is a sequence of content units arranged in such a way that the learning of each unit may be accomplished as a single act provided the capabilities described by specific prior units (in the sequence) have already been learned by the learner." To illustrate the intent of his definition, Gagné provides several analyses of curricula, one of which concerns mathematics. The notable feature here is the hierarchy of content units which he proposes. The determination of this sequence is crucial. Each unit of content has prerequisites which must be identified and ordered so that the curriculum, in a real sense, is a unified whole.

How accurately these hypothetical sequences of content units can be portrayed is always a problem. The "pass-fail" procedure proposed by Gagné for establishing and checking the hierarchy of content certainly has promise. He emphasizes that this method does not provide evaluation of a curriculum, but rather provides evidence as to whether a given hypothesized sequence is pedagogically reasonable or feasible. In any event, in some ways it offers important implications for the national program for the assessment of educational progress described by Tyler. It seems reasonable to assume that the hierarchy of units of content provides an important key to the Tyler proposal to determine the achievements that all, or almost all, students have acquired, those which the most advanced have learned, and those which the "average" students have learned. The mastery tests needed to obtain this information could be a direct outgrowth of the "pass-fail" approach based on the hierarchy of content units.

Rather than define the term "curriculum," Scriven prefers to speak of "educational instruments." These are processes, personnel, procedures, programs, and the like that are operative when formal educational activities take place. This means that the curriculum, for example, is not viewed in the abstract, but is put to use. Necessarily, interactions exist. Content units, teachers, and the teaching environment are principal factors which interact, often in an ill-defined manner, when a curriculum is actually used.

If content units are not to be evaluated in an abstract way, but rather in a reasonably typical situation, then these and many other interactions exist. Evaluation of such a program in the last analysis must mean a situation which is dynamic and creative. Hence, Scriven's use of the expression "educational instruments" suggests a highly realistic situation. At the same time, methodology problems with respect to curriculum evaluation become difficult because of the involvement of teachers, students, and a teaching environment which are idiosyncratic.

EVALUATION STRATEGIES

In an important way, the position we face today with regard to the evaluation of educational instruments is centered on the question of choice of strategies. Scriven makes a serious effort to classify some of the major possibilities in this regard. He establishes a number of differentiations such as those between evaluation goals and evaluation roles, those between formative evaluation and summative evaluation, and those between intrinsic evaluation and pay-off evaluation. The usefulness of these differentiations may vary with the individual evaluator concerned with a particular problem. It is difficult to believe, however, that they will fail to assist in the process of clarifying some of the issues faced now with regard to evaluating educational instruments.

Consider for a moment the differentiation between evaluation goals and evaluation roles. Evaluation goals are attempts to answer

science curriculum development. Paper read at the Regional Conference of the National Science Teacher's Association, Milwaukee, October 1, 1965.

Ausubel, D. P. Psychological aspects of curriculum evaluation. Paper read at the National Seminar for Research in Vocational and Technical Education, University of Illinois, 1966.

Banta, C. O. Sources of data for program evaluation. *Adult Education, 5,* 1955, 227-230.

Barr, A. S., et al. Wisconsin studies of the measurement and prediction of teacher effectiveness. *Journal of Experimental Education, 30,* 1961, 5-156.

Bellack, A. A. *Theory and research in teaching.* New York: Bureau of Publications, Teacher's College, Columbia University, 1963.

Benson, C. S. *The economics of public education.* Boston: Houghton Mifflin, 1961.

Berelson, B. The state of communicative research. *Public Opinion Quarterly, 23,* 1959, 1-6.

Berg, H. D. (Ed.) *Evaluation in social studies.* 35th Yearbook. Washington, D. C.: National Council for the Social Studies, 1965.

Birkmaier, Emma. Evaluating the foreign language program. *The North Central Association Quarterly, 40,* 1966, 263-271.

Bloom, B. S. (Ed.) *The role of the educational sciences in curriculum development.* Chicago: University of Chicago, 1964. (mimeograph)

Bloom, B. S., Englehart, M. D., Furst, E. J., Hill, W. H., and Krathwohl, D. R. *A taxonomy of educational objectives: Handbook I, the cognitive domain.* New York: Longmans, Green, 1956.

Board of Education of Baltimore County. *A Guide for evaluating elementary schools.* (revised) Towson, Md.: Baltimore County Board of Education, 1963.

Brickell, H. M. State organization for educational change: a case study and a proposal. In Miles, M. B. (Ed.), *Innovation in Education.* New York: Bureau of Publications, Teacher's College, Columbia University, 1964.

Britton, L. M. *Report of visitations and sources investigated.* "Operation Yardstick" report to the Martha Holden Jennings Foundation. Cleveland: the Foundation, 1964.

Broudy, H. S., Smith, B. O., and Burnett, J. R. *Democracy and excellence in American secondary education.* Chicago: Rand McNally, 1964.

Brown, B. B. Bringing philosophy into the study of teacher effectiveness. *The Journal of Teacher Education, 17,* 1966, 35-40.

Brownell, W. A. The evaluation of learning under dissimilar systems of instruction. R. L. Thorndike Award Paper, American Psychological Association, Chicago, 1965.

Bruner, J. *The process of education.* Cambridge: Harvard University Press, 1960.

Byrn, D., et al. *Evaluation in extension.* U. S. Federal Extension Service. Topeka, Kansas: H. M. Ives, 1959.

Cahen, L. S. An interim report on the national longitudinal study of mathematical abilities. *The Mathematics Teacher, 18,* 1965, 522-526.

Campbell, D. T., and Fiske, D. W. Convergent and discriminant validation by the multitrait-multimethod matrix. *Psychological Bulletin, 56,* 1959, 81-105.

Carlson, R. O., et al. *Change processes in the public schools.* Center for the Advanced Study of Educational Administration, University of Oregon, 1965.

Carroll, J. B. School learning over the long haul. In J. D. Krumboltz (Ed.), *Learning and the Educational Process.* Chicago: Rand McNally, 1965.

Cawelti, G. *Guide for conducting an evaluation of the comprehensive high school through faculty self-study.* Chicago: North Central Association, 1966.

Christal, R. E. *JAN: a technique for analyzing group judgment.* Lackland AFB, Texas: Technical Documentary Report PRL°TDR-63-3, February, 1963, 1965. 6570th Personnel Research Laboratory, Aerospace Medicine Division, Air Force Systems Command.

Clark, D. L., and Guba, E. G. An examination of potential change roles in education. Paper read at the Symposium on Innovation in Planning School Curricula, Airlie House, Virginia, October, 1965.

Commager, H. S. Our schools have kept us free. *Life,* 29, October 16, 1950, 46-47.

Committee on Tax Education and School Finance. *Does better education cost more?* Washington, D. C.: National Education Association, 1959.

Conant, J. B. *The American high school today.* New York: McGraw-Hill, 1959.

Corey, S. *Action research to improve school practices.* New York: Bureau of Publications, Teacher's College, Columbia, 1953.

Cox, R. C. Item selection techniques and evaluation of instructional objectives. *Journal of Educational Measurement, 2,* 1965, 181-186.

Cox, R. C., and Graham, G. T. The development of a sequentially scaled achievement test. Paper delivered at Annual Meeting, American Educational Research Association, Chicago, February, 1966.

Crawford, W. R. *A validation of the structure and generality of "A Taxonomy of Intellectual Processes."* Unpublished doctoral dissertation, Florida State University, 1966.

Cronbach, L. J. Course improvement through evaluation. *Teacher's College Record, 64,* 1963, 672-683.

Cronbach, L. J. The logic of experiments on discovery. In Shulman, L. M., and Keislar, E. (Eds.), *Learning by discovery.* Chicago: Rand McNally, 1966.

Cronbach, L. J. Psychological issues pertinent to recent American curriculum reform. Paper read at the 14th International Congress of Applied Psychology, 1961.

Cronbach, L. J., and Gleser, G. C. *Psychological tests and personnel decisions.* (2nd ed.) Urbana: University of Illinois Press, 1964.

Diederich, P. B., French, J. W., and Carlton, S. T. Factors in judgment of writing ability. Princeton, N. J.: *ETS Research Bulletin,* 1961.

Downey, L. W. *The task of public education: the perceptions of people.* Chicago: Midwest Administration Center, University of Chicago, 1960.

Dressel, P. L. *Evaluation in the Basic College at Michigan State University.* New York: Harper, 1958.

Dressel, P. L. Teaching, learning, and evaluation. *Improving College and University Teaching, 13,* 1960, 11-15.

Dressel, P. L., et al. *Evaluation in higher education.* Boston: Houghton Mifflin, 1961.

Dressel, P. L., and Mayhew, L. B. *General education: explorations in evaluation.* Washington, D. C.: American Council on Education, 1954.

DuBois, P. H., and Wientge, K. M. *Strategies of research on learning in educational settings.* St. Louis: Washington University, 1964.

Dyer, H. S. *Tentative proposal for an experiment to assess the need for a special test of BSCS biology in the College Board Admissions Testing Program.* Princeton: Educational Testing Service, 1964.

Dyer, H. S. The discovery and development of educational goals. *Proceedings of the 1966 International Conference on Testing Problems.* Princeton: Educational Testing Service. (in press)

Easley, J. A., Jr. Evaluation problems of the UICSM curriculum project. Paper read at the National Seminar for Research in Vocational Education, University of Illinois, 1966.

Ebel, R. L. *Measuring educational achievement.* New York: Prentice-Hall, 1965.

Educational Policies Commission. *An essay on quality in public education.* Washington, D. C.: National Education Association, 1959.

Educational Policies Commission. *The central purpose of American education.* Washington, D. C.: National Education Association, 1961.

Educational Testing Service. *A plan for evaluating the quality of educational programs in Pennsylvania—highlights.* Princeton: the Service, 1965.

Eisner, E. W. *Educational objectives: help or hindrance.* Paper read at the annual meeting of the American Educational Research Association, Chicago, February, 1966.

Engleman, F. E., Cooper, Shirley, and Ellena, W. J. *Vignettes on the theory and practice of school administration.* New York: Macmillan, 1963.

Epperson, D. C., and Schmuck, R. A. An experimentalist critique of programmed instruction. *Educational Theory, 12,* 1962, 247-254.

Ferris, F. L. Testing in the new curricula: numerology, tyranny, or common sense. *School Review, 20,* 1962, 112-131.

Findley, W. G. (Ed.) *The impact and improvement of school testing programs.* 62nd Yearbook, Part 2. Chicago: National Society for the Study of Education, 1963.

Findley, W. G. The ultimate goals of education. *The School Review,* January, 1956, 10-17.

Flanagan, J. C., et al. Studies of the American high school. Report to the U. S. Office of Education, Cooperative Research Project No. 226. Pittsburgh: Project TALENT Office, University of Pittsburgh, 1962.

Flanagan, J. C., et al. The American high-school student. Report to the U. S. Office of Education, Cooperative Research Project No. 635. Pittsburgh: Project TALENT Office, University of Pittsburgh, 1964.

Flanders, N. A. Analyzing teacher behavior. *Educational Leadership, 19,* 1961, 173-180.

Ford, G. W., and Pugno, L. (Eds.) *The structure of knowledge and the curriculum.* Chicago: Rand McNally, 1964.

Forehand, G. The role of the evaluator in curriculum research. Pittsburgh: Carnegie Institute of Technology, 1963. (typescript)

Frederiksen, N. Proficiency tests for training evaluation. In Glaser, R. (Ed.), *Training Research and Education.* Pittsburgh: University of Pittsburgh Press, 1962.

Freeman, F. N. *How children learn.* Boston: Houghton Mifflin, 1917.

Freeman, L. C., et al. *Metropolitan decision-making: further analyses from the Syracuse Study of Local Community Leadership.* Syracuse: University College of Syracuse University, 1956.

French, W., et al. *Behavioral goals of general education in the high school.* New York: Russell Sage Foundation, 1957.

Gage, N. L. (Ed.) *Handbook of research on teaching.* Chicago: Rand McNally, 1963.

Gagné, R. M. The acquisition of knowledge. *Psychology Review, 69,* 1962, 355-365.

Gagné, R. M. The analysis of instructional objectives for the design of instruction. In Glaser, R. (Ed.), *Teaching machines and programmed learning. II: Data and directions.* Washington, D. C.: National Education Association, 1965, 21-65 (a).

Gagné, R. M. *The conditions of learning.* New York: Holt, Rinehart, and Winston, 1965 (b).

Gagné, R. M. Educational objectives and human performance. In Krumboltz, J. D. (Ed.), *Learning and the educational process.* Chicago: Rand McNally, 1965, 1-24 (c).

Gagné, R. M. (Ed.) *Learning and individual differences.* Columbus, Ohio: Chas. E. Merrill Books, 1966.

Gagné, R. M., and Staff, University of Md. Mathematics Project. Some factors in learning non-metric geometry. *Monographs of the Society for Research in Child Development, 30,* 1965, 42-49.

Gagné, R. M., and Bassler, O. C. Study of retention of some topics of elementary non-metric geometry. *Journal of Educational Psychology, 54,* 1963, 123-131.

Gagné, R. M., Mayor, J. R., Garstens, H. L., and Paradise, N. E. Factors in acquiring knowledge of mathematical tasks. *Psychological Monographs, 76,* 1962, (Whole No. 526).

Gagné, R. M., and Paradise, N. E. Abilities and learning sets in knowledge acquisition. *Psychological Monographs, 75,* 1961, (Whole No. 518).

Gardner, J. W. *Excellence.* New York: Harper and Row, 1961.

Gardner, W. E., and Warmke, R. F. Evaluating programs in economic education. *Social Education, 30,* 1966, 244-246.

Gerber, J. *The evaluation of the 1962 English Institute.* New York: Modern Language Association, 4 Washington Place, 1964.

Gerken, C. d'A. Registry examination data feedback in physical therapy education. *Archives of Physical Medicine and Rehabilitation,* March, 1959, 91-98.

Gibson, Eleanor J. Learning to read. *Science, 148,* 1965, 1066-1072.

Gibson, J. S. *New frontiers in the social sciences; goals for students, means for teachers.* Medford, Mass.: Lincoln Filene Center for Citizenship and Public Affairs, 1965.

Glaser, R. Some research problems in automated instruction: instructional programming and subject matter structure. In Coulson, J. E. (Ed.), *Programmed learning and computer-based instruction.* New York: Wiley, 1962, 67-85.

Glaser, R. Instructional technology and the measurement of learning outcomes. *American Psychologist, 18*, 1963, 519-522.

Glaser, R., Damrin, Dora E., and Gardner, F. M. The TAB item: a technique for the measurement of proficiency in diagnostic problem-solving tasks. Urbana: Bureau of Research and Service, College of Education, University of Illinois, 1952.

Golden, W. M. UICSM in its second decade. *Journal of Research in Science Teaching, 1*, 1963, 265-269.

Goode, D. The centrality of evaluation. *Improving College and University Teaching, 13*, 1960, 16-18.

Goodlad, J. G. *School curriculum reform in the United States.* New York: Fund for the Advancement of Education, 1964.

Gordon, I. J. The assessment of classroom emotional climate by means of the observation schedule and record. *Journal of Teacher Education, 18*, 1966, 224-232.

Grambs, J. D., et al. *The junior high school we need.* Washington, D. C.: National Education Association, 1961.

Gray, D. J. *The 1965 Institute in English.* New York: Modern Language Association, 4 Washington Place, 1966.

Grobman, Hulda. Student performance in new high school biology programs. *Science, 143*, 1964, 265-266.

Guba, E. G., and Getzels, J. W. Personality and teacher effectiveness: a problem in theoretical research. *Journal of Educational Psychology, 46*, 1955, 330-344.

Guild, R. E. The criterion problem in evaluation of instructors. Seattle: Department of Psychology, University of Washington, 1966. (mimeograph)

Guttman, L. A basis for scaling qualitative data. *American Sociological Review, 9*, 1944, 139-150.

Hahn, M. E. *Psychoevaluation: adaptation—distribution—adjustment.* New York: McGraw-Hill, 1963.

Halpin, A. W., and Croft, D. B. *The organizational climate of schools.* Report submitted to the U. S. Office of Education, Cooperative Research Project No. SAE 543 (8939). Cooperative Research, Salt Lake City: University of Utah, 1963.

Harris, C. W. (Ed.) *Problems in measuring change.* Madison: University of Wisconsin Press, 1963.

Hastings, J. T. Innovations in evaluation for innovations in curriculum. In Steinberg, E. R., et al., *Curriculum development and evaluation in English and the social studies.* Pittsburgh: Carnegie Institute of Technology, 1964.

Hastings, J. T. Curriculum evaluation: the whys of the outcomes. *Journal of Educational Measurement, 3*, 1966, 27-32.

Heath, R. W. Pitfalls in the evaluation of new curricula. *Science Education, 46*, 1962, 216.

Heath, R. W. Curriculum, cognition, and educational measurement. *Educational and Psychological Measurement, 24*, 1964, 239-253. (a)

Heath, R. W. (Ed.) *New Curricula.* New York: Harper and Row, 1964. (b)

Hively, W. II. *Defining criterion behavior for programmed instruction in elementary mathematics.* Cambridge, Mass.: Committee on Programmed Instruction, Harvard University, 1963.

Hively, W. II. Constructing, evaluating, and revising a program of instruction in algebra for in-service teacher training: a case history and an essay on methodology. Minneapolis: Minnesota National Laboratory, 1964.

Hovland, C. Reconciling conflicting results derived from experimental and survey studies of attitude change. *American Psychologist, 14,* 1959, 8-17.

Hovland, C. I., Lumsdaine, A. A., and Sheffield, F. D. *Experiments on mass communication.* Appendices: measurement problems encountered. Princeton: Princeton University Press, 1949.

Husén, T. Curriculum research in Sweden. *International Review of Education, 11,* 1965, 189-208.

Hyman, H. H., et al. *Applications of methods of evaluation: four studies of the encampment for citizenship.* Berkeley: University of California Press, 1962.

Institute of Administrative Research. *A study of public opinion about schools.* New York: the Institute, 1956.

James, H. T. *Wealth, expenditures, and decision-making for education.* Report to the U. S. Office of Education, Research Contracts Division, Project No. 1241. Palo Alto: Stanford University, 1963.

Johnson, M., Jr. Definitions and models in curriculum theory. Ithaca: School of Education, Cornell University, 1966. (multilith)

Joint Committee on Programed Instruction and Teaching Machines, *Criteria for Assessing Programed Instructional Materials.* 1962 interim report of the Joint Committee, NDEA Title 7. *Audiovisual Instruction,* February, 1963, 84-89.

Jongeward, R. E. *Factors in supporting and evaluating state-aided experimental programs.* Paper presented at annual meeting of American Educational Research Association, 1965.

Judd, C. H. Analysis of learning processes and specific training. *National Education Association Addresses and Proceedings,* 1921, 783-786.

Jung, C., Lippitt, R., Fox, R., and Chesler, M. Retrieving social science knowledge for secondary curriculum development. Publication No. 109, Social Science Education Consortium, Lafayette, Ind.: Purdue University, 1966.

Kelley, T. L. *Crossroads in the mind of man.* Stanford, Calif.: Stanford University Press, 1928.

Kerlinger, F. N. Attitudes toward education and perceptions of teacher characteristics: a study. *American Educational Research Journal, 3,* 1966, 159-168.

Kersh, B. Y. Programming classroom instruction. In Glaser, R. (Ed.), *Teaching machines and programmed learning. II: data and directions.* Washington, D. C.: National Educational Association of the United States, 1965, 321-368.

Kershaw, J. A., and McKean, R. N. *Systems analysis and education.* Report to the Ford Foundation, RM-2473-FF. Santa Monica, Calif.: Rand Corporation, 1959.

Kimbrough, R. *Political power in educational decision making.* Chicago: Rand McNally, 1964.

Kleinman, J., and Hannen, C. *Profiles of excellence.* Washington, D. C.: National Education Association, 1966.

Knolle, L. M. *Identifying superior teachers.* New York: Institute of Administrative Research, 1959.

Knox, A. B. Developing an evaluation plan in adult farmer education. *Agricultural Education Magazine,* December, 1962, 110 ff.

Krathwohl, D. R. Stating objectives appropriately for program, for curriculum, and for instructional materials development. *Journal of Teacher Education, 12,* 1965, 83-92.

Krathwohl, D. R., Bloom, B. S., and Masia, B. B. *Taxonomy of educational objectives. Handbook II: Affective domain.* New York: McKay, 1964.

Kropp, R. P., and Stoker, H. W. *The construction and validation of tests of the cognitive processes as described in the "Taxonomy of Educational Objectives."* Report to the U. S. Office of Education, Cooperative Research Project No. 2117, 1966.

Kurland, N. D. Developing indicators of educational performance. Paper read at the 31st Educational Conference, Educational Records Bureau, October, 1966.

Lennon, R. T. Assumptions underlying the use of content validity. *Educational and Psychological Measurement,* 1955, 294.

Leton, D. A. Criterion problems and curriculum evaluation. Paper read at the National Seminar for Research in Vocational and Technical Education, University of Illinois, 1966.

Lindquist, E. F. (Ed.) *Educational measurement.* Washington, D. C.: American Council on Education, 1951.

Lindvall, C. M. (Ed.) *Defining educational objectives.* Pittsburgh: University of Pittsburgh Press, 1964.

Lortie, D. C. Administrator, advocate, or therapist? *Harvard Educational Review, 35,* 1965, 3-17.

MacDonald, J. B., and Raths, J. D. Curriculum research: problems, techniques, and prospects. *Review of Educational Research, 34,* 1963, 29-32.

Madden, J. M. An application to job evaluation of a policy-capturing model for analyzing individual and group judgment. Lackland Air Force Base, Texas: 6570th Personnel Research Laboratory, Aerospace Medical Division, 1963.

Maier, M. S. Evaluation of a new mathematics curriculum. Princeton: Educational Testing Service, 1962.

Martin, Jane R. Can there be universally applicable criteria of good teaching? *Harvard Educational Review, 33,* 1963, 484-491.

Mason, J. I. *Usage—one measure of quality education.* Pittsburgh: Tri-State Area School Study Council, 1958.

McGuire, Christine H., and Babbott, D. Simulation technique in the measurement of problem-solving skills: a technological or conceptual innovation. *Journal of Educational Measurement,* 1966. (in press)

McKeachie, W. J. *The appraisal of teaching in large universities.* Ann Arbor: University of Michigan, 1959.

Merwin, J. C. The progress of exploration toward a national assessment of educational progress. *Journal of Educational Measurement, 3,* 1966, 5-10.

Merwin, J. C., and Gardner, E. F. Development and application of tests of educational achievement. *Review of Educational Research, 32,* 1962, 40-50.

Messick, Samuel. The perceived structure of political relationships. *Sociometry, 24,* 1961, 270-278.

Meux, M., and Smith, B. O. Logical dimensions of teaching behavior. Urbana: Bureau of Educational Research, University of Illinois, 1961. (mimeograph)

Miles, M. B. (Ed.) *Innovations in education.* New York: Bureau of Publications, Teacher's College, Columbia University, 1964.

Miller, G. A., et al. *Plans and the structure of behavior.* New York: Holt, Rinehart, and Winston, 1960.

Miller, H. L., and McGuire, Christine. *Evaluating liberal adult education.* Chicago: Center for the Study of Liberal Education for Adults, 1961.

Mitzel, H. E. Teacher effectiveness. In Harris, Chester W. (Ed.) *Encyclopedia of Educational Research.* New York: Macmillan, 1960, 1481-1491.

Morrissett, I. (Ed.) *Concepts and structure in the new social science curricula.* West Lafayette, Ind.: Social Science Education Consortium, 427 Wood St., 1966.

Mort, P. R., and Furno, O. F. *Theory and synthesis of a sequential simplex: a model for assessing the effectiveness of administrative policies.* New York: Institute of Administrative Research, 1960.

National Citizen's Council for Better Schools. *Yardsticks for public schools.* Evanston: National School Boards Association, 1959.

National Education Association. *Factors basic to good educational outcomes.* Research memo 1964-15. Washington, D. C.: the Association, 1964.

National Education Association. *How good are your schools?* Washington, D. C.: the Association, 1958.

National School Boards Association and the American Association of School Administrators. *Quest for Quality Series.* Washington, D. C.: National Education Association, 1960.

National Study of Secondary School Evaluation. *Evaluative criteria: 1960 edition.* Washington, D. C.: the Study, 1960.

National Study of Secondary School Evaluation. *Evaluative criteria for junior high schools.* Washington, D. C.: the Study, 1963.

Neidt, C. O. *Changes in attitudes during learning.* Report to the U. S. Office of Education. Title VII Project No. C-1139, 1964.

New England School Development Council. New England educational data systems. *The NESDEC News, 17,* February, 1964 (whole issue).

New Jersey School Development Council. *A survey of teacher evaluation guides.* New Brunswick, N. J.: Graduate School of Education, Rutgers, 1962.

Newton, J. M., and Hickey, A. E. Sequence effects in programmed learning of a verbal concept. *Journal of Educational Psychology, 56,* 1965, 140-147.

New York State Education Department. *School quality workbook.* Albany: the Department, 1963.

Ohio Association of School Administrators. *Quality education.* Columbus: Policy and Research Committee, the Association, 1964.

Ohio Department of Education. *A guide for self-appraisal of the elementary school.* Columbus: State of Ohio, 1961.

Ohio Legislative Service Commission. *Ohio's high schools: a statistical profile.* Staff Research Report No. 56. Columbus: State of Ohio, 1963.

Osgood, C. E., Suci, G. J., and Tannenbaum, P. H. *The measurement of meaning.* Urbana: University of Illinois Press, 1957.

Pace, C. R. When students judge their college. *College Board Review, 58,* Winter, 1965-66, 26-28.

Page, E. B. The imminence of grading essays by computer. *Phi Delta Kappan, 47,* 1966, 238-243.

Payette, R. F. Report of the School Mathematics Study Group curriculum evaluation. Princeton: Educational Testing Service, 1961.

Pellegrin, R. J. Community power structure and educational decision-making in the local community. Paper read at the 1965 National Convention of School Administrators, Atlantic City, 1965.

Pellegrin, R. J. Analysis of sources and processes of innovation in education. Eugene: Center for the Advanced Study of Educational Administration, University of Oregon, 1966. (mimeograph)

Phenix, P. H. *Realms of meaning.* New York: McGraw-Hill, 1964.

Restle, F. *Psychology of judgment and choices: a theoretical essay.* New York: Wiley, 1961.

Rogers, E. M. Toward a new model for educational change. Paper read at the Conference on Strategies for Educational Change, Washington, D. C., 1965.

Rosenbloom, P. C. (Ed.) *Modern viewpoints in the curriculum.* New York: McGraw-Hill, 1964.

Rosenbloom, P. C. Effectiveness of the SMSG material for grades 7-12. Pub. No. 36-B-288. Minneapolis: State Department of Education, 1962.

Ryans, D. G. *Characteristics of teachers.* Washington, D. C.: American Council on Education, 1960.

Sawin, E. L., and Smith, J. F. Curriculum evaluation. *Improving College and University Teaching, 14,* 1966, 81-86.

Scheffler, I. Justifying curriculum decisions. *The School Review,* December, 1958, 470-472.

Schutz, R. E. Report of the AERA 1966 Presession on Experimental Design. Tempe: Arizona State University, 1966.

Schutz, R. E., Baker, R. L., and Gerlach, V. S. *Measurements procedures in programmed instruction.* Tempe: Classroom Learning Laboratory, Arizona State University, 1964.

Scriven, M. The philosophy of science in educational research. *Review of Educational Research, 30,* 1960, 422-429.

Scriven, M. Student values as educational objectives. *Proceedings of the 1965 Invitational Conference on Testing Problems.* Princeton: Educational Testing Service, 1965.

Shuff, R. V. A comparative study of achievement in mathematics at the seventh and eighth grade levels under two approaches, School Mathematics Study Group and traditional. Unpublished doctoral dissertation, University of Minnesota, 1962.

Silverman, R. E. The evaluation of programmed instruction: a problem in decision-making. *Psychology in the Schools, 1,* 1964, 74-78.

Simpson, R. H., and Seidman, J. M. *Student evaluation of teaching and learning.* Washington, D. C.: American Association of Colleges for Teacher Education, 1962.

Sizer, T. R. Classroom revolution: reform movement or panacea? *Saturday Review*, June 19, 1965, 52 ff.

Sjoberg, L. Thurstonian methods in the measurement of learning. *Scandinavian Journal of Psychology*, 6, 1965, 33-48.

Smith, E. R., and Tyler, R. W. *Appraising and recording student progress*. New York: Harper and Row, 1942.

Smith, W. I., and Moore, J. W. *Learning sets in programmed instruction*. Final Report, U. S. Office of Education Grant No. 7-48-0070-208, March, 1965.

Squire, J. R. Evaluating high school English programs. *The North Central Association Quarterly*, 40, 1966, 247-254.

Stake, R. E. The countenance of educational evaluation. Urbana: University of Illinois Center for Instructional Research and Curriculum Evaluation, 1966. (mimeograph)

Stanley, J. C. *Measurement in today's schools*. (4th ed.) Englewood Cliffs, N. J.: Prentice-Hall, 1964.

Steinberg, E. R., Fenton, E., Forehand, G. A., and Slack, R. C. Curriculum development and evaluation in English and social studies. Report to the U. S. Office of Education, Cooperative Research Project No. F-041. Pittsburgh: Carnegie Institute of Technology, 1964.

Stephan, F. F., and McCarthy, P. J. *Sampling opinions, an analysis of survey procedure*. New York: Wiley, 1958.

Stone, P. J. An introduction to the General Inquirer: a computer system for the study of written or spoken material. Cambridge, Mass.: Laboratory of Social Relations, Harvard University, 1964.

Street, D. Sociological aspects of curriculum development. Paper presented at the National Seminar for Research in Vocational and Technical Education, University of Illinois, 1966.

Stufflebeam, D. L. Evaluation under Title I of the Elementary and Secondary Act of 1965. Paper read at the Evaluation Conference sponsored by the Michigan State Department of Education, East Lansing, January, 1966.

Sullivan, H. A taxonomy of instructional objectives. Tempe: Classroom Learning Laboratory, Arizona State University, 1966. (mimeograph)

Taba, Hilda. *Curriculum development: theory and practice*. New York: Harcourt, Brace, and World, 1962.

Taylor, P. A. The mapping of concepts. Unpublished doctoral dissertation, University of Illinois, 1966.

Taylor, P. A., and Maguire, T. O. A theoretical evaluation model. *The Manitoba Journal of Educational Research*, 1, 1966, 12-17.

Taylor, P. A., and Maguire, T. O. Perceptions of some objectives for a science curriculum. Urbana: University of Illinois Center for Instructional Research and Curriculum Evaluation, 1966.

Thomas, M. J. *A guide for action: improving public education through citizen participation*. Pittsburgh: University of Pittsburgh Press, 1965.

Thompson, J. M. Teachers, history, and NDEA institutes, 1965. American Council of Learned Societies, April, 1966.

Torgerson, W. S. *Theory and methods of scaling*. New York: Wiley, 1958.

Trott, J. R. The evaluation of clinical teaching and teachers. Winnipeg: Faculty of Dentistry, University of Manitoba, 1966. (Xerox)

Troyer, M. E., and Pace, C. R. *Evaluation in teacher education.* Washington, D. C.: American Council on Education, 1944.

Trump, J. L. *New directions to quality education: the secondary school tomorrow.* Washington, D. C.: National Association of Secondary School Principals, 1960.

Tucker, L. R. Factor analysis of relevance judgments: an approach to content validity. *Proceedings of the 1961 Invitational Conference on Testing Problems,* Princeton: Educational Testing Service, 1961.

Tyler, R. W. *Constructing achievement tests.* Columbus, Ohio: Ohio State University, 1934.

Tyler, R. W. The functions of measurement in improving instruction. In Lindquist, E. F. (Ed.), *Educational Measurement,* Washington, D. C.: American Council on Education, 1950.

Tyler, R. W. The evaluation of teachers and teaching. In Cooper, R. M. (Ed.), *The two ends of the log,* Minneapolis: University of Minnesota Press, 1958, 164-176.

Tyler, R. W. *Some persistent questions on the defining of objectives.* Pittsburgh: University of Pittsburgh Press, 1964, 77-83.

Tyler, R. W. The objectives and plans for a National Assessment of Educational Progress. *Journal of Educational Measurement, 3,* 1966, 1-4.

U. S. Office of Education. *Guidelines: special programs for educationally deprived children: Section II, design and evaluation of projects.* No. OE-35079. Washington, D. C.: U. S. Government Printing Office, 1965.

University of Kentucky Bureau of School Service. *The measure of a good school.* Lexington: the Bureau, 1964.

Walbesser, H. H. Evaluation as a guide to course improvement. *Science Education News,* November, 1964, 1-2.

Walbesser, H. H. Science curriculum evaluation: observations on a position. *The Science Teacher, 33,* 1966.

Walcott, C. On evaluation. *ESS Newsletter.* Watertown, Mass.: Educational Services, Inc., February, 1965.

Webb, E. J., et al. *Unobtrusive measures: nonreactive research in the social sciences.* Chicago: Rand McNally, 1966.

Weinberg, J. S. State aid to education in Massachusetts. Cambridge: New England School Development Council, 1962.

Weisbrod, B. A. Conceptual issues in evaluating training programs. Madison: University of Wisconsin, (Author), 1966.

Wessell, N. Y. Innovation and evaluation: in whose hands? *Proceedings of the 1966 Invitational Conference on Testing Problems.* Princeton: Educational Testing Service. (in press)

Wherry, R. J., and Naylor, J. C. Comparison of two approaches—JAN and PROF—for capturing rater strategies. *Educational and Psychological Measurement, 26,* 1966, 267-286.

Wiles, K., and Patterson, F. *The high school we need.* Commission on the Education of Adolescents, Association for Supervision and Curriculum Development. Washington, D. C.: National Education Association, 1959.

Williams, B. R. Economics in unwonted places. *Advancement of Science,* January, 1965, 431-438.

Williams, J. D. Teaching methods, research background, and design of experiment. National Foundation for Educational Research in England

and Wales, The Mere, Upton Park, Slough, Bucks, England: *Arithmetic Research Bulletins I, II, and III*, 1965. (mimeo)

Woodrow, H. A. The ability to learn. *Psychology Reviews, 3,* 1946, 147-158.

Wrightstone, J. W., Justman, J., and Robbins, I. *Evaluation in modern education.* New York: American Book, 1956.

PRINTED IN U.S.A.